Operation Exodus

Gustav Scheller
with
Jonathan Miles

Sovereign World

Sovereign World Limited
PO Box 777
Tonbridge
Kent TN11 0ZS
England

Scripture quotations are taken from the New King James Version,
copyright © 1983 by Thomas Nelson Inc.

ISBN: 1 85240 226 1

This Sovereign World book is distributed in North America
by Renew Books, a ministry of Gospel Light, Ventura,
California, USA. For a free catalog of resources from Renew
Books/Gospel Light, please contact your Christian supplier or
call 1-800-4-GOSPEL.

Cover pictures: Ebenezer Emergency Fund
Typeset by CRB Associates, Reepham, Norfolk.
Printed in England by Clays Ltd, St Ives plc.

Dedication

To my precious wife, Elsa, travel companion, prayer partner, and wise counsellor. Next to God's grace, you are the best thing that ever happened to me.

To Beverley Hill, trusted and loyal assistant over many years, whose support has been an inspiration to me.

To all the valiant servants of Ebenezer, past and present, who have shown love in action to God's chosen people.

To the many believers who have accompanied us in prayer. Without their faithful intercession Operation Exodus would not have succeeded.

To all those who with their gracious and often sacrificial giving have enabled Jews to return to the Promised Land.

Contents

The Authors

Gustav Scheller

Gustav Scheller was born in Switzerland in 1929 and was called into the Lord's presence on 18th February 2000. He came to the UK over 40 years ago to build up a travel and tour operating company. Gustav established foreign language schools and at the peak of the company's business had offices in London, Edinburgh, Switzerland and Tokyo. The company received the Queen's Award to Industry for travel and tourism in 1974.

Gustav married Elsa, who was a tremendous support to him in his work for Ebenezer Emergency Fund. Elsa continues to be actively involved in the work.

In 1982, when attending Bible College in the USA, the Lord revealed to Gustav and Elsa, through the prophetic Word, His plan and purpose for the return of His chosen people to the Promised Land. He also showed them that the time would come when they would personally be involved with the *aliyah* in a practical way.

On their return from Bible College, Gustav and Elsa began a ministry called 'Let My People Go' (God's command to Pharaoh, through Moses). This ministry provided practical help and comfort to the Jewish people in the then USSR and also brought to the attention of the Church the plight of the Jewish people in that land.

It was during an International Prayer Conference in Jerusalem in 1991 – the middle of the Gulf War – when 120 intercessors from many different nations had gathered to pray for Israel that the Lord spoke to Gustav and told him that **now** was the time to bring home His people from the disintegrating Soviet Union. It was not a time Gustav himself would have chosen!

Thus Ebenezer Emergency Fund was born and Gentile believers worldwide have responded with prayer and financial support. 'Ebenezer' is spoken of in the Book of Samuel, and the name means 'Thus far has the Lord helped' – and this is our testimony because without His help, we can do nothing. Originally the assistance was in the form of mercy flights, followed in late 1991 and early 1992 by three trial sailings from Odessa to Haifa. This proved to be an important milestone, as never before in modern history has a shipping route been established between the former Soviet Union and Israel. The Lord made it possible!

The work has since expanded and Ebenezer Emergency Fund completed its 120th sailing in December 2000. Ebenezer Emergency Fund has helped over 70,000 of God's chosen people to go home from many parts of the former Soviet Union. The Lord has shown that we should carry home His sons and daughters from the ends of the earth. So Ebenezer teams are seeking out Jews in some of the most far-flung places of the former Soviet Union and helping them to reach the Promised Land.

> *'See, I will beckon to the Gentiles, I will lift up My banner to the people; they will bring your sons in their arms and carry your daughters on their shoulders.'*
>
> (Isaiah 49:22)

We know that not one of God's promises to Israel have failed. He has kept them, every one. **He who scattered Israel will gather them and keep them** and bring them back to the Land He has given their forefathers as an everlasting possession.

Jonathan Miles

Jonathan Miles is a journalist who has lived in Israel for ten years and, together with his wife and five children, worked with Jewish immigrants and Arab refugees.

Foreword

It was during our first International Prayer Conference in Jerusalem back in 1985 that we felt the Lord's calling to go to the land of the north, the then Soviet Union, to pray on location for the release of Jews to return to the Promised Land. We went that year and in 1986, but we did not know how we could be involved in a more practical way. Then in 1991, when we had a most unusual prayer conference in Jerusalem during the first week of the Gulf War, I got a big surprise. Gustav Scheller came up to me one morning and said he had been given the green light from the Lord to start helping to bring back Jewish people from the Soviet Union.

I looked at him in astonishment. Didn't he realize that this was the most inconvenient time to even talk about this? Who among the Jewish people would like to return to a nation that was being bombarded with Saddam Hussein's Scud missiles? And how would we be able to arrange for transporting Jews right in the middle of a war situation? I was tempted to reject the whole idea, but instead found myself saying to Gustav: 'Yes, I believe this is of the Lord!' I was just as shocked over my own words as I was over Gustav's proposal.

Soon afterwards Operation Exodus began. In under ten years we have helped to bring back over 70,000 Jews to Israel from the former Soviet Union by plane and by ship. This amazing story has happened, and continues to happen, because the prophetic scriptures declare that the Gentiles would carry the sons and daughters of Zion back to their own land (Isaiah 49:22).

Operation Exodus largely happened because one man heard the voice of God and obeyed Him. On 18th February 2000, Gustav Scheller, founder of Ebenezer Emergency Fund and author of this book, was called into the presence of his Lord and Messiah, bringing the pioneering phase of Operation Exodus to an end. Gustav came into full-time service for the kingdom of God rather late in life but in a relatively short time has accomplished more than many others who have spent a lifetime in ministry. He put all his business skills and, more importantly, all his passion and love for the Jewish people to establish, with his dear wife, Elsa, one of the fastest-growing Christian ministries today.

May God use this new edition of a remarkable story to wake up His Church world-wide to the need of getting involved in bringing the Jewish people back to the Promised Land not only from the former Soviet Union but from all over the world.

Johannes Facius
Chairman
Ebenezer International
January 2001

Publisher's Introduction

In order to understand this book it is first of all essential to understand God, His nature and character, and His eternal purposes for Israel.

Out of love He **chose** Abraham, Isaac and Jacob, whose name was changed to Israel, and promised them a land of their own (Genesis 12:1; 15:7). It is clearly defined as being *'from the river of Egypt to the great river, the river Euphrates'* (Genesis 15:18). That promise has yet to be fulfilled in its completeness, but one day God will ensure that His covenant is kept in full.

We live in an age of 'equality'. Some people even consider it unfair that God should choose the Jewish people as His special people, or indeed promise them their land for ever. Such a promise was made to no other nation. God also foreknew that they would be in Egypt 400 years and told Abraham so:

> *'Know certainly that your descendants will be strangers in a land that is not theirs, and will serve them and they will afflict them four hundred years.'*
> (Genesis 15:13)

God promised that afterwards they would come out and enter the Promised Land. This was achieved through Moses and is the first exodus. It is important to understand this as God later refers back to it in describing a second exodus, which clearly confirms there are two, one past, one future, i.e. after the prophecy which postdates the first exodus.

When we then trace Jewish history it is important to understand God's covenant with them, especially the Deuteronomy 28 covenant. It is in two sections. Verses 1–14 describe the blessings of obedience; however, verses 15–68 describe in great detail the consequences of disobedience. History tells us that tragically they disobeyed God's laws. The Israelites therefore experienced the consequences of that choice. Specifically:

> *'And you shall become an astonishment, a proverb, and a byword among all the nations where the LORD will drive you.'*　　　(Deuteronomy 28:37)

> *'... you shall be plucked from off the land which you go to possess. Then the LORD will scatter you among all peoples, from one end of the earth to the other ...'*
> (Deuteronomy 28:63–64)

God's people disobeyed Him many times, and caused God's anger to rise up, yet even when He allowed them to go into captivity for a time under Nebuchadnezzar (6th century BC), that exile was both temporary and limited, i.e. to Babylon only. They came back. The second exodus we shall look at later cannot be the Babylonian exile for two very simple reasons.

Firstly, the Jewish people were not scattered all over the earth. They were taken into exile into Babylon.

Secondly, Babylon is **east** of Israel, and the second exodus is from 'the land of the north.' The old Soviet Union, now Russia, lies due north of Israel.

> *'... they shall come together out of the land of the north to the land that I have given as an inheritance to your fathers.'* (Jeremiah 3:18)

So how did they get there?

History tells us that just before Pilate turned Jesus over to the Roman soldiers to be crucified, the chief priests and elders had goaded the crowd to such a frenzy that they cursed themselves: *'His blood be on us and on our children'* (Matthew 27:25). In AD 70 the Roman Emperor Titus came and sacked Jerusalem, scattering the Jewish people across the earth. God dispossessed His people of their land. Remarkably, they maintained their identity for almost 2,000 years, experiencing all the curses of Deuteronomy 28, until God chose to give them back their land, and bring back His chosen people. The State of Israel was reborn in 1948, which in itself is a miracle. It has survived war after war, and the process of immigration still continues to this day.

Unfortunately many Christians wrongly believe that because God rejected His people for a time, He abandoned them for ever, and the Covenant promises passed to the Church. And so we had 'replacement theology' – replacing Israel with the Church. While it remains true that the Church became partakers of the covenants and God's promises, it is nevertheless equally true that God has not, did not, and will not ever abandon Israel as His chosen people, even at times of discipline.

Jeremiah 31 gives Israel the most wonderful promise:

> *'Yes, I have loved you with an everlasting love;*
> *Therefore with lovingkindness I have drawn you.*
> *Again I will build you, and you shall be rebuilt.'*
> (Jeremiah 31:3–4)

> *'Behold I will bring them from the north country,*
> *And gather them from the ends of the earth.'*
> (Jeremiah 31:8)

> *'He who scattered Israel will gather him.'*
> (Jeremiah 31:10)

These prophecies have never been fulfilled in full. In order to make the the point unequivocally, God links His faithfulness to the very existence of the earth:

> *'Thus says the LORD,*
> *Who gives the sun for a light by day,*
> *And the ordinances of the moon and the stars for a*
>   *light by night...*
> *If those ordinances depart*
> *From before Me, says the LORD,*
> *Then the seed of Israel shall also cease*
> *From being a nation before me forever.'*
> (Jeremiah 31:35–36)

God then repeats it, to emphasise the certainty:

'If heaven above can be measured,
And the foundations of the earth searched out
*   beneath,*
I will also cast off the seed of Israel
*For all that they have done, says the L*ORD*.'*

(Jeremiah 31:37)

Clearly the sun and moon have not ceased shining, so God declares that Israel will remain a nation before Him forever.

During all that time from AD 70 to AD 1948 Israel remained a nation in God's eyes. Then something happened. The United Nations voted to partition Palestine, thus creating the State of Israel in May 1948.

The nation was reborn. The Jewish people **were back** in their land, with their own identity, territory and language. It truly was the hand of God. But history has not ceased, nor has opposition to God's purposes in history. Despite all attempts to strangle the new nation at birth Israel prevailed, and has done so, despite on-going attempts to destroy her. But God has not finished with His people. The wonder is that He has plans for Israel, and is watching over His chosen people. He will bring them back to their land and fulfil every promise made.

There will be a second exodus, back from oppression to their homeland. It will be even more significant than the first exodus from Egypt:

'"Therefore behold, the days are coming," says the L*ORD*, "that it shall no more be said, 'The L*ORD *lives*

*who brought up the children of Israel from the land of Egypt,' but, 'The L*ORD* lives who brought up the children of Israel from the land of the north and from all the lands where He had driven them.' For I will bring them back into their land which I gave to their fathers."'* (Jeremiah 16:14–16)

Firstly, they will come through 'fishing' and encouragement. Afterwards persecution will drive them home. They will be hunted (Jeremiah 16:16). Expect to see anti-Semitism increasing. Right now God is fishing. This book tells but a part of what God is doing, and how He is using the Ebenezer Fund to fulfil His purposes. We are witnessing history being made before our eyes. It is time for the Church to be challenged into action. It is time to love God's chosen people as the prophetic fulfilment of God's plan for their homecoming takes place.

Chapter 1

'I am God, and there is none like Me,
Declaring the end from the beginning,
And from ancient times
things that are not yet done.'

(Isaiah 46:9–10)

My first inkling of these strange events came in the dining room of a hotel in the north of England. It was the hour of the evening meal and I took the only unoccupied place. The gentleman opposite me, I learned as we waited for the food to be served, was a doctor and a believer.

'I've just come from Israel,' he told me. My ears pricked up. In that spring of 1982 my wife Elsa and I had just finished ten weeks of Bible study at the beautiful Christian Retreat in Bradenton, Florida, and our eyes had been opened to God's promises to the Jewish people. I didn't fully understand why, but I had a sense that Elsa and I should go to Israel. I had come aside to the hotel for a few days to seek further direction.

'I was at the Feast of Tabernacles in Jerusalem,' the doctor was continuing, 'and heard a man named Steve Lightle share the most amazing vision the Lord gave him of the forthcoming exodus of Jews from the Soviet Union.'

I nearly jumped up right there. The doctor looked surprised at my excitement. But I'd been reading about this very thing in the prophets, and now he told me it was happening!

I had no peace until I could get to Jerusalem and look for Steve Lightle. 'Lord,' I prayed, 'if this man is still in Israel, let me meet him. I want to know more about his vision.'

✤ ✤ ✤

Elsa and I flew to Israel's Ben Gurion Airport two weeks later and took a taxi directly to our hotel in Jerusalem. Early the next morning we went for a walk and I pondered how we might find Steve. He had directed the European work of the Full Gospel Businessmen's Fellowship International. While I'd never met him personally I did hear him speak once before a crowd of 8,000 at a world convention in New Orleans. With his distinctive nose and curly grey hair it was easy to see that he himself is Jewish.

To my utter amazement just then I saw a man who looked like Steve walking the other way across the street.

'Steve, Steve!' I shouted over the traffic. He looked our way but didn't recognize us and started to walk on.

'No, Steve, you don't know us, but we know you. I must meet you.' Elsa and I hurried across the street and caught up to him – the first person we met in Israel! 'We want to hear more about your vision,' I told him, and he agreed to meet us the following evening for dinner.

It turned out to be an exhilarating night. Elsa and I forgot our meal as Steve shared what happened during a six-day fast in 1974. 'The power of God came in the room. It was so strong I couldn't get off the floor ... On the last day I got up and sat in a large overstuffed chair. I saw a giant screen with a multitude of Jewish faces. There were so many of them. There were hundreds of thousands of Jewish people. They were on the screen and I began to see them as they began to come together and to mill around. And I could see their faces just as I can see you across the table. And then I saw the nation they were within, and it was the Soviet Union. I could see the borders of that land. I'm sitting there watching this. This is something new. Nothing like this has ever happened to me before.

'They came together to one place, and there then appeared a highway that God Himself went and built. Nobody could get on that highway except whom the Lord permitted, and these Jewish people. They got on this specially-built highway and they began to walk and they began to come forth. And at the same time God raised up men with ministries as great or greater than that of Moses, who went to the authorities in the Soviet Union and proclaimed to them, "Thus saith the LORD God of Israel, 'Let My people go!'"

'And the authorities refused and wouldn't. Their hearts became hardened and they would not let the people go. And prophecies began to come, and plagues and judgment began to come against the

Soviet Union until they were brought to their knees, that whole nation. And they just coughed up all these people on that highway. God built it and those Jews, hundreds of thousands of them, began to walk out.'

It sounded incredible, but Elsa and I had already begun to glimpse confirmation in the Scriptures. I knew I had more to learn and decided to remain in the country for a few weeks after Elsa returned to our children in England. Steve and his wife Judy graciously invited me to stay at their home in Ein Kerem, birthplace of John the Baptist.

Steve was exuberant, with an infectious laugh, overflowing with the joy of the Lord. As we sat around the kitchen table, instead of reading a newspaper Steve read the word of God aloud to his family in a full voice. It was such a beautiful time, a time of learning and growing in the Word. I found that the final ingathering of the Jewish people was foretold by all the major prophets – appearing in over a hundred passages (see Appendix 3) – with a special emphasis on the return from 'the land of the north' (see Jeremiah 3:18, 16:15, 23:8, 31:8 and Zechariah 2:6).

Then I saw in Isaiah 49:22 God's declaration that the Gentiles would carry home the sons and daughters of the Jewish people. I was sitting there reading and suddenly realized, **You must be part of it**. It just electrified me.

Steve had only spoken of his vision publicly a handful of times in the past nine years. He would always wait on the Lord to direct him; otherwise he wouldn't take a step. But now he felt it was time to proclaim it widely, and as I watched him I realized that he had been given a message for the Church.

'One day I met a man by the name of David Pawson,' he told me. David is a well-known pastor and Bible teacher in England. 'And he looked at me and said, "God has a calling on your life. You have a prophetic role to fulfil, and Steve, you have **got** to obey God!"

'I'll tell you,' he continued. 'In the Spirit it was as though somebody grabbed hold of me and started shaking me. It was just so powerful.'

I invited Steve to Bournemouth, the coastal town two hours south-west of London where Elsa and I lived and my business was based. As I was looking at the diary back in England the only day which was free was Ascension Day, May 12th, 1983. 'Lord,' I said, 'I think we should have a public meeting.' And somehow I felt we should take the Town Hall, one of the largest halls in town with capacity for up to 1,000 persons.

So I said to my secretary Beverley, 'Try this. If we can get the Town Hall we will take it as a sign that it is of the Lord.'

She came back into my office shortly and said, 'Yes. The Town Hall – we can have it.'

I made a provisional booking. But then I began to doubt. The Christians in our area knew little about Israel. It was unheard of at that time to fill a hall with a meeting about Jews going home. 'Lord, what am I doing?' I thought. 'We'll need 1,000 people there. I'll make a fool of myself if I bring Steve to an empty hall.'

'Lord,' I said again. 'If this is your will, then please arrange for someone to phone me with a word from Scripture as confirmation.'

I had an option which allowed me to reserve the hall for two weeks before making payment. Every day I expected something to happen, but not so. On the Sunday night before the option expired I sat in my study until midnight. I thought the phone had to ring. I was so sure we would have confirmation.

The phone didn't ring. At midnight I finally said to Elsa, 'First thing tomorrow I'll give back the Town Hall. We'll go to a church and have a low-profile meeting.'

As I was getting out of bed early the next morning the phone rang. It was a lady I didn't know well, but I respected her as a godly woman. She said, 'Gustav, I have a word from the Lord for you. I've been in prayer about the Town Hall. Would you look at Romans 10:15?'

I read it and it said,

> *'And how shall they preach unless they are sent? As it is written:*
>> *"How beautiful are the feet of those who preach the gospel of peace,*
>> *Who bring glad tidings of good things!"'*

It was a total surprise. I was amazed and relieved. Joyfully that morning I confirmed the Town Hall booking and advertised the event to the local churches.

The night before the meeting, when I came home from the office Elsa met me at the door. 'We just had a phone call from Switzerland,' she said. Our oldest son Martin was living there with his lovely wife Debra, and from the look on Elsa's face I knew something had happened.

'Martin collapsed at work,' she went on. 'He had to go to the hospital for an emergency operation.'

I had no words. It was such a shock. We were deeply troubled, not knowing what had happened. Perhaps a heart attack. Our first thought was for one of us to go at once. Steve, who was staying with us, was less perturbed. Of course it wasn't his son – but he was sure it was a spiritual attack on our meeting.

The next day we gathered in our home with others who were helping at the Town Hall that night. We fell to our knees in prayer. After some time I opened my eyes. All 25 in the room were either kneeling or flat on their faces before the Lord. It was such a mighty prayer meeting. Two words came to us:

'Your son will be healed within days – and you will light a fire for the return of the Jews that will spread through the length and breadth of the British Isles.'

Elsa and I had the peace of the Lord to stay and go on with the meeting. At the Town Hall that night we were stunned. It was filled to capacity. People had driven for hours to attend. The atmosphere was electric.

'The Lord is here with us tonight,' I said from the platform before introducing Steve. 'I wouldn't be in any other place than in the Lord's hands with God's people tonight.'

Steve came and related his vision as we had first heard it in Jerusalem. Then he paused.

'I might say right now, if anybody wants to leave,

you're perfectly welcome to leave at this moment. If you don't, you're going to be just as responsible for what you're going to hear as I am.'

Five seconds passed. You could have heard a pin drop. Nobody moved.

'This to my knowledge is the first time this message has been publicly shared within the UK. And I will tell you something: **This will go through your whole nation** ... to every person in the land, so that nobody, nobody will ever be able to say, "Well, that was a freak accident of history." No! Everybody shall know what the Lord God is going to do.'

'I want to read to you one representative set of Scriptures out of Jeremiah 23,' Steve continued. Each person had received at the door a list of many of the great ingathering Scriptures: Deuteronomy 30; Isaiah 11, 35, 43; Jeremiah 3, 16, 23, 30, 31; Ezekiel 36–39; Zephaniah 3. 'Let's understand something of what God wants to do in the last days. Why is it so prophetic for us here tonight? Why are the Jews of the Soviet Union so prophetic to God in the last days? Why is God beginning to place them on the hearts of believers around the whole world? And not only believers, but now I'm meeting Jewish people and God has spoken to their hearts what He's going to do with the Jews of the Soviet Union.

> ' "But I will gather the remnant of My flock out of all countries where I have driven them, and bring them back to their folds; and they shall be fruitful and increase. I will set up shepherds over them who will feed them; and they shall fear no more, nor

24

*be dismayed, nor shall they be lacking," says the
LORD.*

"Behold, the days are coming," says the LORD,
"That I will raise to David a Branch of
righteousness;
A King shall reign and prosper,
And execute judgment and righteousness in the
earth.
In His days Judah will be saved,
And Israel will dwell safely;
Now this is His name by which He will be called:

THE LORD OUR RIGHTEOUSNESS." '

(Jeremiah 23:3–6)

'What is the prophet telling us?' Steve continued.
'He's saying, "Listen. There is a day coming in the
history of the world – God is going to gather His
ancient people, the Jewish people, back from the four
corners of the earth. And when they are gathered
back and when they are returned to the land, **then** I
shall raise up the righteous Branch." And He shall
come forth, not as a lamb led to the slaughter, but He
shall come as the King of kings, He shall come as the
Lord of lords.

'And brothers and sisters, **that** is the second
coming of the Lord Jesus, and when He comes all
the Jewish people of the world, from all the countries
to which He's scattered them, shall be back in Israel.
He's not coming back to a land that's vacant of His
ancient people. He's coming back and it's going to be
full of the ancient people of God. For it will be the

fulfilment of the prophecy of Zechariah chapter 12 verse 10: *"And they shall behold Him whom they pierced."* And the weeping that's going to come – but I'll tell you then it'll be turned to tears of joy. You're going to see an explosion that only God can orchestrate by His Holy Spirit.

'Now how can I make such a bold statement as that? God does things prophetically. Before Jesus came there was one called John the Baptist that went forth with a voice crying in the wilderness: *"Prepare ye the way of the Lord."* He was the prophetic preparation for the Messiah to come. And when Jesus comes again He will have a prophetic preparation and it is the return of the Jews from around the world.

'But it begins in a specific nation. How do we know? Let's go on to verse 7: *" 'Therefore . . . ' "* It is a conjunction. It relates back to these prior verses.

> *' "Therefore, behold, the days are coming," says the LORD, "that they shall no longer say, 'As the LORD lives who brought up the children of Israel from the land of Egypt,' but, 'As the LORD lives who brought up and led the descendants of the house of Israel from the north country and from all the countries where I had driven them.' And they shall dwell in their own land." '*   (Jeremiah 23:7)

'There is only one nation to the north of Israel today that has any sizable number of Jews in it. That is the Soviet Union. 2.1 million Jewish people in the Soviet Union according to the latest estimates.

'God is going to give an opportunity to the nations of the world to bless His people, no matter what nation they're in, and it is to help them return to Israel. That's what we're doing here tonight. If your heart is open to hear the truth of God, take these verses, go to your prayer closet, and say, "God, is this true?"'

None of us were the same after the message of that night. Many in the audience had never heard what the Bible says about the return of the Jews. 'It was an eye-opener to have those Scriptures pointed out,' one woman said. 'I must have read them without understanding.' Israel just wasn't a topic in our churches. We'd always thought of the passages in the Bible about Israel only as teaching illustrations for application in our own lives.

The promised fire was lit – and when Elsa flew out the next day to Switzerland, she found our son was indeed already recovering from what doctors said was a collapsed lung.

✣ ✣ ✣

So Steve and I teamed up and travelled together to bring this message to the Church in the UK. I recall those days so well. 'It's time that somebody began to tell the leadership of the Soviet Union what the word of the Lord says,' Steve declared everywhere we went. 'Either they bow their knee to God, or God is going to judge them. One or the other.' Following a news conference at the Finnish parliament the BBC World Service broadcast the challenge across the globe. One of the major Soviet newspapers mocked it under the headline 'God Brings Russia to its Knees.'

Even the believers would look at us with big eyes in

these meetings and think we were funny guys. It seemed impossible to believe in 1983 that communism would fall and the Jews be released; it was the height of the Cold War. The Soviet Union was at the peak of its military power and world influence, expanding its empire into places like Afghanistan, Nicaragua, and Angola. A vigorous Yuri Andropov, who headed the KGB for 15 years and directed the harassment and imprisonment of Jews wishing to emigrate, had taken the reins of power when Leonid Brezhnev died just six months before the Town Hall meeting.

None of us realized it but the wheels of judgment had already started to turn. From 1979 on the Soviet grain harvests were so disastrous the authorities simply stopped reporting the statistics. Heavy rains spoiled the planting; withering heat stunted the growing season; then heavy rains returned at harvest time to flatten crops and leave those still standing sodden. In Moscow, Marxist historian Roy Medvedev in an article headlined 'Why the Russians Can't Grow Grain' reached the conclusion that 'in agriculture, 50% depends on God.'

The unthinkable was happening: a modern industrialized superpower faced famine. A call went out to the public to conserve food. To prevent starvation the Soviet leadership was forced to spend nearly half of its annual hard currency earnings on food imports – just as there was a sharp rise in military spending by the United States under Ronald Reagan. Squeezed from both sides, the Soviet Union was approaching bankruptcy.

Then one morning 15 months after Andropov took power Moscow awoke to funereal music on the radio. After hours of speculation the world was told: Andropov – despite recent Kremlin assurances of his good health – was dead. He was succeeded by Konstantin Chernenko, age 72 but still a year younger than his counterpart Reagan.

Thirteen months later classical music returned to the radio in Moscow in place of a comedy program. The next afternoon came the stunning news that Chernenko too was dead. Brezhnev, Andropov, and Chernenko, all gone in less than two-and-a-half years. Until then the average tenure of a general secretary had been nearly 20 years! The deaths of the two shortest-serving rulers in Soviet history cleared the way for the meteoric rise of a younger, lesser-known man named Mikhail Gorbachev.

✣ ✣ ✣

During this period Steve and I, together with international intercessory leaders Johannes Facius and Kjell Sjöberg, called a conference in Jerusalem for believers to pray for Israel and the release of Soviet Jewry. There it was agreed that Steve, Johannes, and two other intercessors would make a prayer journey through the Soviet Union in April to prepare the way for the coming exodus. It was purely an exercise in faith. Less than 100 Jews a month were then allowed to emigrate. Over 360,000 who had dared to apply were refused, even as the Communist Party told the world 'all who want to leave have already gone.' Anatoly Sharansky, leader of the emigration movement, was in his seventh year in a labour camp for 'treason and anti-Soviet agitation.'

The intercessors arrived a month after Gorbachev took power and travelled to all the major Jewish centres in the Soviet Union. In each place they encircled at least one of the many giant statues of Lenin, praying and proclaiming that this idol would fall. They sought out traffic points – airports, seaways, rail stations – and prayed that the Lord would open them up for sending Jews back to Israel. At the Ukrainian Black Sea port of Odessa they fanned out across the massive Potemkin staircase leading from the city down to the port, and went slowly down the steps praying. At the bottom they turned and went back up doing the same – nearly bumping into their KGB tails.

Such on-site spiritual warfare was at the time rather unusual. Back at their hotel over coffee the men laughed and admitted they felt foolish for what they were doing. 'What do we hope to accomplish by this?' asked Johannes, his faith lingering. Back home others in his church shared his scepticism.

And in fact during his first nine months as general secretary Gorbachev proved just as obstinate toward the Jews as his predecessors. He told French television interviewers that Jews enjoy more 'political and other rights' in the USSR than in any other country, and trotted out the party line that only those who 'know state secrets' are prevented from leaving. Challenged about Anatoly Sharansky, Gorbachev declared that he had 'breached our laws and was sentenced by court for that.'

At the end of the year Steve and Johannes returned to the USSR, this time with a team of 13 other intercessors from France, Sweden, Finland, the US, and Germany. Their mission: to proclaim judgment on the pharaoh who still refused to let God's people go. By resisting God's timing for fulfilment of His word, they believed the Soviet Union had entered on a collision course with the Almighty Himself and had to be broken. 'We have a feeling God is putting an end to this whole thing,' Johannes said. The team prepared with three days of prayer and fasting in Finland, taking the theme from Jeremiah 51 of judgment and devastation coming on the land.

On the bitter cold afternoon of December 31 they proclaimed outside Gorbachev's office in Moscow the words Samuel once spoke to Saul: *'Because you have rejected the word of the LORD, He has rejected you as king. The LORD has torn the kingdom from you today.'*

The intercessors then crossed Red Square, walking along the fortress walls of the Kremlin and praying in the Spirit. A Finnish pastor pointed to the top of a tower where a great red star was illuminated against the darkening afternoon sky.

'What does that mean?' he asked the group.

'It's a symbol of man and the strength of man,' said a Swedish member who specialized in occult and New Age research. 'The communist system represents trust in man. The Soviets worship scientific achievement. But Jeremiah 17:5 says, *"Cursed is the man who trusts in man and makes flesh his strength."'*

The men continued to walk and pray. 'I have a sense of that star falling down,' one said after a few

31

minutes, the others nodding in agreement. 'And it will happen very soon.'

That night the group came together at their hotel. 'Listen to what it says in Revelation eight!' one of the team exclaimed, opening his Bible. 'A star falling from heaven. This is what we were praying about today.'

At midnight the group went down to the Moscow river beside the Kremlin and, following the instructions to an intercessor in Jeremiah 51:59–64, took a Bible marked with passages of judgment, tied it to a large stone, and threw it through the thin ice covering the river. 'Thus the Soviet Union shall sink and not rise from the catastrophe that I will bring upon her,' they declared in the name of the LORD.

'Everything seemed so crazy,' one of the men said afterwards, 'impossible to the human mind. But we knew God was in it.'

✤ ✤ ✤

Four months later came the event which sent shock waves through the Soviet Union and the world: the explosion and uncontrolled fire at the Chernobyl nuclear reactor in the Ukraine. The accident emitted as much long-term radiation into the world's air, topsoil, and water as all nuclear tests and bombs ever exploded. Local and regional Communist Party officials attempted to cover up what was happening, sending their own children away while ordering others to march in May Day celebrations even as a lethal radioactive cloud hung over the region.

Thousands suffered from headaches, coughing, and spitting of blood. Only when the cloud rained down

contamination on Poland, the Scandinavian countries, and beyond, did the story begin to leak out.
Eventually hundreds of thousands of residents were
permanently evacuated from the Chernobyl region –
too late. Many had been exposed to enough radiation
to kill them over the coming years, as were an
unknown number of the 600,000 workers sent in for
the massive clean-up attempt. When the full truth
came out it tore the mask from the face of the
communist leadership and more than any other
factor caused the people to lose faith in the Soviet
system.

Left contaminated was a huge swathe of the Soviet
Union's premier farming region and water supply. In
a failing effort to prevent contamination of the
groundwater, deep wells were sunk around Chernobyl
and airplanes treated the clouds above to limit rain-
fall. Kiev, the Soviet Union's third largest city just
over 100 kilometres to the south, was forced to
develop an alternative water supply. Because of lake
contamination limits were put on the consumption
of sweet water fish in Finland, and increased radiation
was detected in rainwater as far away as the east coast
of the United States.

Then within a few months of the disaster came a
startling realization, as reported on the front page of
The New York Times in a July 26, 1986 dispatch from
Moscow:

> 'A prominent Russian writer recently produced a
> tattered old Bible and with a practised hand
> turned to Revelation.

"Listen," he said, "this is incredible."

> *"And the third angel sounded, and there fell a great star from heaven, burning as it were a lamp, and it fell upon the third part of the rivers and upon the fountains of waters; and the name of the star is called wormwood: and the third part of the waters became wormwood; and many men died of the waters, because they were made bitter."*

In a dictionary he showed the Ukrainian word for wormwood, a bitter wild herb used as a tonic in rural Russia: chernobyl.

The writer, an atheist, was hardly alone in pointing out the apocalyptic reference to the star called chernobyl. The discovery had spread across the Soviet land with uncanny speed.'

None but God knows the connection between the Revelation passage and Chernobyl, between the intercession of the Church and the disaster which came upon the Soviet Union. But of the significance of Chernobyl there is no question. 'It shook us greatly,' Gorbachev said looking back years later. 'It was a turning point.' *Glasnost* (openness) would be the result, coupled with the *perestroika* (restructuring) which sought to deal with the Soviet Union's ongoing economic crisis.

The iron gates which held the Jews were starting to shake. And we remembered Steve's words at the Town Hall: 'Nobody, nobody will ever be able to say, "Well, that was a freak accident of history." No!'

Chapter 2

'This is what the Sovereign LORD says:
"See, I will beckon to the Gentiles,
I will lift up My banner to the peoples;
They will bring your sons in their arms
And carry your daughters on their shoulders." '

(Isaiah 49:22 NIV)

During the following years the intercessory prayer conference in Jerusalem became an annual event, and I took care of the practical arrangements. Eventually I found myself praying 'Lord, have I served enough tables?' I knew he had promoted the deacons of old to spiritual works as well. 'I just don't want to be a Stephen, Lord!'

I will never forget what happened when I sat across a hotel breakfast table in Jerusalem from Bill Styles, a Baptist minister who was working as a travel agent in Israel. He looked at me intently and said, 'I had a dream two months ago. And in this dream I was standing in a huge terminal surrounded by many people, old and young, poorly-dressed, with their luggage at their sides. I realized they were Jews. Nobody seemed to know what to do. Then I noticed a man came in dressed in a business suit. He had white hair and was carrying a briefcase. He knew what to do.

'And the Lord spoke to me that I would help this man in bringing Jewish people home from the ends of the earth. As soon as I saw you this morning, I recognized you. I can tell you, it was you I saw in the dream.'

It was as if the Lord would hit me over my head and ask me, 'How many times do I have to tell you? One day you will help the Jews from the land of the north to go home.'

Waiting for things has never been my strength; but in a way I knew the vision was for the appointed time. The Lord began to prepare me by gently weaning me from the business I'd built up over the years since coming to England from Switzerland.

As Elsa will testify, at one time I had been married to my work. I brought in overseas visitors and opened language schools for them in Oxford, Cambridge, London, Torquay, and Bournemouth, as well as travel offices in a number of cities around Britain. My business expanded and I eventually opened offices in Switzerland, Japan, and the US, with representatives in many other countries. As the market leader in incoming tourism I received the Queen's Award to Industry and was invited to Buckingham Palace. My secret ambition was to be knighted one day.

All this changed on a wet and misty Sunday in the autumn of 1979, when Elsa, our four children, and I dressed up and trooped off to church, a lifelong ritual in keeping with my upbringing. There was a new minister at the Winton Methodist Church, and on this morning I was surprised to see him open the pulpit to a group of ordinary lay people. They stood at the front of the old stone church and shared simply from their own lives how God had touched them.

It was as if I heard it for the first time. I called myself a Christian, and I could be found warming the same pew each Sunday – but the other six days of the week I lived the way I wanted. Now I was challenged to hear that only by repentance could I be a child of God.

When they finished speaking they asked for those who would yield their lives to come forward, something that had never happened before in all my years at the church. It was embarrassing – I was the church treasurer – but somehow I knew that I had to get up from my pew. I went down the aisle, past the congregation, and knelt at the communion rail at the foot of a big wooden cross. Tears ran down my cheeks. At age 50 I became a follower of Jesus.

I was too overwhelmed to speak when I returned to where Elsa was sitting and felt her hand take mine. I could see she was stunned and thrilled. She had prayed for this for years.

Alone in my study that night I picked up the Living Bible, which fell open to the story of the prodigal son in Luke 15. One phrase stood out as though illuminated:

> *' "This son of mine was dead and has returned to life. He was lost and is found." So the party began.'*

I sensed that my new life would bring joy and

fulfilment which, despite my worldly success, I had not yet experienced.

Over the following months my business, which had done so well over many years, started to crumble. It was the time of the oil crisis, high inflation and high interest rates. Travel came almost to a standstill, and I found I had over-expanded the work. After much agonizing, I had to lay off 80 of my permanent staff of 220. It really burdened me. I spoke to each man and woman myself and lifted them up in prayer.

Still the company went down. Many days I sat at my desk calculating how many days and weeks remained before I had to put the whole business into liquidation. My life's work was coming to the abyss – all would collapse. I was proud of my achievements. All my life I'd been building up. But now there was nothing I could do. I was just helpless, fighting against a brick wall.

On my 51st birthday I tried something I'd never done before. I asked the Lord to give me a word. Elsa and I were starting each day with a reading from a book of Scripture texts called *Daily Watchwords*, born out of a powerful visitation of the Holy Spirit in 1727 to a community of persecuted Moravian believers who had taken refuge in the village of Herrnhut, Germany. Brethren would go from house to house each morning bringing the 'watchword' for the day as a guide to meditation. Eventually the passages for each year were chosen by lot and published in advance. We were now reading from the 250th edition.

That morning's reading was Jesus speaking to Martha:

> *'You are worried and troubled about many things. But one thing is needed.'*

'Yes, Lord,' I confessed, 'I am troubled about the business, the staff, the debts.'

I understood I should release my problems to Him. He was well able to deal with them. 'Lord, give me the chance,' I told Him. 'I want to go before you, I want to really just have this intimate relationship with you. But you must help me.'

I wanted to be entirely sure that this word was for me. Perhaps I wasn't quite ready. In the evening I turned to my American prayer diary – and found exactly the same word assigned for that day. That hit me. It had never happened in all the time we were reading both prayer diaries. I knew God had spoken. I realized He was testing me, and so over a period of time I came to the point of saying, 'Lord, this is your business. I hand it over completely to you. You can do whatever You want with it.'

It took some time to work out this surrender. One can say it – but saying and doing are often two different things in life.

One morning as we were under severe financial pressure I met with an English woman who was my agent in Turkey. She owed me a substantial sum.

'I need this money!' I told her, rapping my fist on the desktop to emphasize each word.

'Mr Scheller, I can't meet my obligations,' she told me. She was desperate. Suddenly I knew I had to help

her. She walked out at the end of the meeting with £1,000 in her pocket.

'I'm going a bit funny,' I told Elsa that night. 'At a time when we can't pay bills and salaries, I'm giving cash away.'

We turned then to our evening reading from Deuteronomy 15:

> *'You shall surely give to* [your poor brother], *and your heart should not be grieved when you give to him, because for this thing the LORD your God will bless you in all your works and in all to which you put your hand.'* (Deuteronomy 15:10)

We had a praise party knowing that I had done the right thing.

I had built in Bournemouth, with the help of a substantial bank loan, a four-storey office block as well as a school with good administrative facilities. I knew that if I could sell one of these buildings I would get a breathing space and the business could return to profitability. But I soon realized that I was not the only one trying to sell an office block; other companies were also in trouble and trying to do the same.

Bournemouth is one of the central points in western England to coordinate bus traffic, and had built a modern administrative block for this purpose. This building caught fire and became unusable. Almost overnight new facilities were needed to continue the work. They took over my building. My business was saved from liquidation.

At the same time it was as if the Lord opened the

tap and business began to flow freely. I can't explain how it happened, but what looked a desperate situation, as weeks went by, turned into a very handsome profit picture. In that year I made more profit than in any other. But the business now truly belonged to the Lord. I realized that I depend on Him, and that not all was due to my own good efforts.

After some years, I had an attractive takeover offer for my language schools, and the Lord reminded me that I had released the business to Him. I felt loyalty to my staff, and told the senior people. They offered instead a management buyout, which I was prepared to gratefully accept.

I was still left with the travel company, but on its own – without the administrative support from the school staff – it began to lose money. I became anxious. We needed the Lord's direction to show a way of escape. I didn't see a way to put it up for sale as it was a losing venture.

Elsa and I started a 'Daniel fast' for three weeks, going without meat and sweets as Daniel and companions had once done in Babylon. Nothing happened. We continued with a full fast for a few days.

And then one morning in the post at home was a very official-looking letter labelled 'Strictly Private'. I picked it up off the floor, intrigued, took it to the breakfast table and opened it first. It was from a consultant who had instructions from a major business house to acquire a travel company. Even though I had given no public indication that I wanted to sell, he had analysed the market and concluded that our company was exactly what they wanted.

I chuckled. Who wants to buy a company that is losing money? 'The Lord has funny ways of dealing with our problems,' I said to Elsa.

A few weeks later I went to London to meet the chairman and finance director. These were top guys, pin-striped suits, in a multi-million pound organization. It was not a good meeting. Somehow I felt we were not speaking the same language. I concluded there would be no deal.

But to my surprise a few days later the chairman drove down to see me at my office in Bournemouth. Above the conference table was a small plaque stating 'Jesus Christ is Lord'. The chairman looked at this and told me, 'I am a Catholic. I studied two years for the priesthood, but realized it was not my calling.'

I just listened, but it established a relationship that was not there before. A mutual trust transpired. 'Make us an offer, including staff details,' he said before leaving. I put one carefully together and sent it off, and a few days later two of his auditors turned up to inspect our books. My heart sank. They would soon realize it was not a profitable venture.

It didn't take long – a phone call came inviting me to the head office. There the chairman said that he wanted to buy the company exactly on the conditions I had submitted! I'll never forget that afternoon when the finance director handed me a letter of intent for the purchase of the company. He stood and just laughed and laughed, and finally said, 'Mr Scheller, I have no clue why we should buy your company.' I laughed too, all the way back to Bourne-mouth – free now for the call the Lord had given me years before.

✣ ✣ ✣

Then came the miracle we had prayed and worked for through the years. As part of Gorbachev's reforms sweeping the Soviet Union, in December 1989 the gates swung open and the Jews were free to leave. Nearly 200,000 rushed out to Israel over the next 13 months. On the eve of our January 1991 prayer conference in Jerusalem a record 35,295 immigrants arrived in one month.

But other events were gripping the attention of the world. Iraqi dictator Saddam Hussein had invaded Kuwait, and was rapidly approaching confrontation with a US-led coalition. If attacked he threatened to 'burn up half of Israel,' understood as a reference to Iraqi missiles capable of reaching Israel with chemical warheads.

The first day of the prayer conference turned out to be the deadline for Iraq to withdraw. Governments warned their citizens to stay out of the region. Most foreign airlines cancelled their flights in and out of Israel, and almost all tourists abandoned their plans to be in the country at the time. But 120 totally-committed Christians from 24 nations turned up at the Holyland Hotel, taking their theme from the biblical call to *'stand in the gap before Me for the land.'*

This group had been sifted. There were many late cancellations, but these were outnumbered by others who were drawn to join us without a previous booking. All knew it could cost their lives. Some had fought to come to Israel against the counsel of family and government. These were real intercessors, wanting to stand with those they prayed for.

As the threat of a massive attack loomed over us the first night we gathered and sang the old hymn 'Great is Thy Faithfulness'. A great strength and peace came over the group and we were absolutely secure in God's hand. We all felt it a privilege and a joy to be in the land at a time like this.

Elsa and I had hardly fallen asleep that night when the telephone jangled by the bedside in our room. The traveller's alarm clock showed 2:15 a.m. Even before picking up the phone I knew – the war had started.

For a moment I was gripped by a sudden burden for the innocent Iraqis who would suffer while Saddam was hidden safely away. Then fully awake I sat up in bed and began making wake-up calls of my own. Within a quarter-hour the long carpeted corridors filled with quietly-talking people. The allied bombardment of Baghdad had begun. 'How will Iraq respond?' was the question I heard on many lips.

Our answer came at the same hour the next night. I was awakened to the ghostly drone of air raid sirens rising, holding a pitch, and slowly receding. American satellites had detected the launching of Iraqi Scud missiles toward Israel – they would land in two minutes.

Elsa and I were sleeping in track suits. We had only to grab the cardboard cartons holding our gas masks and rush to the sealed room on our floor, protected against chemical attack by plastic sheeting taped over the windows and insulation around the door. Others joined us, moving quickly but without panic.

In the room I took off my eyeglasses to put on the gas mask, pulling the elastic straps snug behind my head. I glanced around the room and couldn't help thinking we looked almost more like dogs than humans. We waited for news on the radio of what was happening, each rubbery breath an effort. We couldn't speak to each other but certainly did speak to the Lord.

Nearly two hours passed before a woman's voice came on the radio: 'All residents of Israel may remove gas masks and depart from sealed rooms.'

A spirit of joy erupted and we just began praising the Lord. We heard that missiles with conventional warheads had damaged homes in Tel Aviv and Haifa, but there were no deaths or serious injuries. Messages of encouragement began to come in from believers around the world who were watching these events on television.

The night-time alarms continued throughout the week. It was an emotionally-charged time. I awoke one night when I heard a noise and jumped out of bed.

'*Schatz*,' I cried to Elsa, using our Swiss German term of endearment. 'Can't you hear the siren going?'

She lifted her head from the pillow and cocked an ear. 'No, I don't hear anything.'

Irritated, I opened the window and stuck out my head. I heard only a passing truck.

'Sorry, *schatz*,' I admitted. 'I was wrong.' It was an

exercise we repeated more than once during the week, interspersed with a half-dozen real attacks which we waited out in the sealed rooms.

But even as the missile attacks continued I had the persistent feeling that I was in the right place. There was no anxiety in me or in the group. We knew we were in God's hands. It was the best conference I ever coordinated. There was a unity you only reach at a time of crisis. We moved as an army under a powerful anointing of the Holy Spirit.

We prayed that through the war God would prepare the way for the fulfilment of two biblically-based promises: to bring the gospel to the Muslim world, and bring the children of Israel back to their Promised Land. Many think intercession in these cases is something done only on our knees. But as the conference went on I had an overwhelming sense that God wanted us also to take action: **Now you can begin helping My people to go home**.

I knew Johannes, spiritual leader of the conference, well enough to predict his reaction. 'This is silly,' he would think. 'We're sitting in the basement with gas masks on, talking about bringing Jews under the bombardment of Saddam Hussein.' Johannes and I were usually the most practically-minded of the conference organizers. But somehow I had to go ahead.

I went to Johannes. 'I have the distinct impression,' I told him, 'that now is the time the Lord wants us to help the Jews come home from the land of the north.'

To my amazement, Johannes nodded in agreement.

'Yes – yes, Gustav, I believe this is of the Lord.' We were both so surprised! It was just like God.

Another barrage of missiles landed in Israel at 7:00 a.m. Shabbat morning, and that evening I went before the 120 and shared my impression. To my further amazement, they too unanimously sensed this was a sovereign move of God. They gave an offering for the exodus of Soviet Jewry. With two men I counted it afterwards – and this little group had given $30,000.

We all rejoiced at the confirmation of what God was saying. But if I'd known at the time how things would unfold from there, I probably would have gone into hiding.

Chapter 3

'Who are these who fly like a cloud, And like doves to their roosts?'

(Isaiah 60:8)

'I don't think the prophet Isaiah ever saw an airplane,' Steve quipped. 'The best way he could describe it was a cloud with wings.' At 4:40 a.m. on a Thursday morning four months after the prayer conference, we stood with a small crowd of supporters on the tarmac at Israel's Ben Gurion Airport. The sky was just lightening in the east as the door of a white and blue El Al plane swung open and the first of 250 *olim* (oh-leem – new immigrants, literally 'those going up' to Israel) came down the stairs for their first step on Israeli soil. We saw small children, some clutching dolls and one a small puppy. There were old folks who could hardly make their way down the steps. Some were well dressed, others obviously very poor.

A man went to his hands and knees and kissed the tarmac. The crowd cheered and waved Israeli flags. There was so much excitement. Some *olim* were laughing, some singing, others weeping and spontaneously embracing each other. We felt like Peter at

Pentecost: *'This is that which was spoken by the prophet.'* It was an awesome experience to see them coming for the first time. All that we had talked and prayed about through the 80s we now saw happening with our own eyes.

With the collection from the prayer conference I had turned to the Jewish Agency, the body which until that time organized all *aliyah* (all-lee-ya – immigration, 'going up' to Israel), to see how we could sponsor a flight. We had nothing at the time. There was the prayer conference mailing list of a few hundred names, and a group of about 60–80 believers who would turn out for an evening meeting in Bournemouth. We met in a basement room of a building which Elsa and I called Ebenezer House, after Samuel's testimony in 1 Samuel 7:12 that, *'Thus far the* L<small>ORD</small> *has helped us.'*

We sent out simple material explaining what we felt to do, called it Operation Exodus and set up the Ebenezer Emergency Fund to administer it. I was surprised to get quite a lot of mail in return from people I'd never heard of. But they were so stirred. They knew the Bible and understood the time for the return of God's chosen people had come. One family with three young children wrote me, 'We're not going on holiday this year. It's more important for a Jewish family to go home.' I had never experienced this kind of giving in my life. I sat behind my desk and just wept when I saw how my brothers and sisters were giving.

I got letters daily from Christians who spoke of the love they had for the Jewish people. They wrote,

'Dear Gustav, thank you so much that we can send you this money for a ticket.' It really baffled me. I would read that and think, 'If I gave someone money I would hope they would write a letter to thank me!'

Many of the gifts came from those who had no money. Three blind ladies met in the north of England and saved together to sponsor a passenger. An invalid lady in her sixties living on a pension sent us a letter every month with £2. She took this out of her pension of £49. These really had to be wise keepers of their money. It reminded me more than once of the widow's mite in Luke 21.

Gifts came from Christians in nearly 30 nations. I was astounded at what was happening. A group of about thirty Korean ladies wrote to us. They had no money to give but were praying for us and would contact us later. Their next letter included a cashier's check for $7,500. 'We decided not only to pray,' they wrote, 'but to ask for overtime pay from our jobs – and every penny we received over 30 days went to help the Jewish people home.'

An American couple had started a church in Mexico which grew to 22 congregations. They stood with Israel and God blessed their ministry. 'As I shared the return of the Jews with the poorest of my congregations – people who live in huts with corrugated metal covers as roofs – they decided they wanted to pay for a ticket,' the pastor told me. 'For them even a dollar is a fortune. But they gathered the money together to pay for it.'

The other side which deeply thrilled me was the giving attitude of the Jewish people themselves. The day after our flight arrived, the Israeli government launched an operation to rescue more than 14,000 black Ethiopian Jews, after receiving news of bitter battles between the Ethiopian government and rebels. Forty flights came thundering in during a massive, lightning airlift called Operation Solomon. Five babies were born aboard the aircraft!

Elsa and I visited the Diplomat Hotel in Jerusalem, which the government commandeered and filled with 1,200 of the new arrivals. They had brought no luggage with them, just the clothes they were wearing, the women in their traditional robes. When news of this broke the Jerusalemites filled their cars with clothes, food, medicine, and toys and drove up. Tears came to my eyes when I saw how they welcomed their brothers and sisters. After six hours the police had to barricade the roads leading to the hotel as they were unable to accept any more aid. Romans 11:11 says we should make the Jews jealous; often they have made me jealous.

Elsa and I then went to Budapest to see the Jewish Agency transit camp from which the *olim* had embarked on our flight. The Soviet Union allowed no direct flights to Israel, so all immigrants were first routed through the Eastern European cities of Budapest, Bucharest, or Warsaw. 'Three days ago we had a young girl who was dying of cancer,' the camp director told us. 'She only had a few days to live. After talking it over, we decided she should die in her true homeland.' They found a doctor and nurse and flew her to Israel.

Early the next morning we went with the Agency

team to the central train station in Budapest. As we drove along one of them drew our attention to the Danube river out the window. 'During the Holocaust,' he said quietly, 'members of my family were pushed in and drowned here.' At the train station we learned that Jews were once packed into cattle cars there and sent to the death camp at Auschwitz. Now trains were coming in with *olim* from the Soviet Union.

We walked into the station past a young man kneeling on the ground fiddling with his rucksack, and my escort gave me a little nudge. Instantly I knew this was Israeli security. As we walked around the station I gradually realized there were about half a dozen men in different places. One was reading the paper, but he wasn't really reading, he was watching the movement in the station. There were three trains coming in that day at different hours, and the Russian trains don't run on Swiss time. Often these men had to wait for hours and hours. Elsa and I were deeply impressed by the commitment and sacrifice of the Israeli team.

We went on to sponsor a second and then a third Jewish Agency flight from Budapest, bringing a total of 720 *olim*. But by the time of our third flight in May, I'd begun to get letters from believers reminding me that Isaiah's remarkable vision of Jews returning by air continued with these words:

> *'The ships of Tarshish will come first, to bring your sons from afar, their silver and their gold with them.'*
> (Isaiah 60:9)

'Gustav, what about a ship?' they wrote.

I didn't want to hear about a ship. I knew nothing about ships. It is so much easier to write about ships than to do it. I said, 'Lord, if that is of you I must know from you.'

In early June of 1991 I was talking with a prayer partner in my office, and I brought up all my excuses. 'Listen,' I said. 'This is mission impossible. We would need permits from the Israelis, from the Soviets, from the port authorities. We would need to establish a transit camp to sleep and feed hundreds of people, where it is already difficult just to feed one family. We would have to provide security, we would need a big passenger ship, and we would need an awful lot of money.'

'But,' I said, taking my friend to see a copper plate which had hung on my office wall for years, 'I serve a great God. Look, the Scripture inscribed here says, *"For with God all things are possible"* (Mark 10:27).' As I spoke this out suddenly for the first time I saw there was the image of a ship above the words. Somehow I'd never noticed it before.

It was to me as if the Lord Himself put His hand on my head and said, 'For with Me a ship is possible.' I broke down and wept. All doubt vanished.

Almost immediately I left for Jerusalem, full of joy. I'd learned through the years, 'When the Lord speaks, I run.' If I wait then doubts come. He wants us to trust Him, even if we think it's absolutely crazy – His ways are so much higher than ours.

I went alone to the big stone headquarters of the Jewish Agency. I hoped they would cooperate with us in some way, perhaps release *olim* from their network to travel on a ship. I climbed the staircase to the second floor executive corridor, walked past the photos of the century's great Zionists, and came to an office where two senior officials were waiting for me.

I thanked them for the good cooperation we'd enjoyed in working on the flights. 'Now the time has come to take this a step further,' I said, picking up my Bible.

'This is **your** Bible,' I told them, 'the word of the living God. And the prophet Isaiah says here that your people will return by air **and** by ships. We'd like to work with you on opening a sea route to Israel.'

The two looked at each other and smiled. They were still gracious – we had paid for flights and there was a good chance we would continue to do so – but there certainly wasn't the same interest in helping with a ship.

They gave a word of caution to dampen my enthusiasm. 'Others have tried and failed. There hasn't been a direct route from the Soviet Union – for flights or sailings – since the establishment of the state.'

We shook hands and I walked back down the corridor of power, down the staircase, and out into the hot summer sun.

'They think it's a crazy idea,' I realized, 'that will fizzle out, and I will come to my senses.'

I shared their reaction with Elsa afterwards. 'They are happy to accept our financial contributions, but hadn't counted on us wanting hands-on involvement.'

'They're so strong, so set in themselves,' she said, 'it must seem amusing for nobodies like us from the outside to come and tell them how to bring Jews home.'

Everywhere I turned I wasn't well received. There were no takers willing to come alongside. Doors were slammed in my face one after the other. Even among Christians in Jerusalem I didn't initially find any great enthusiasm for this project. I was a bit shaken. Maybe I had illusions that they would all stand ready to welcome me.

For three days in my Jerusalem apartment the Lord made me withdraw from the outside world, praying, fasting, seeking His face. I was quite miserable. On one side I was pregnant with a ship. There was no question about it. But I didn't see any breakthrough, and unlike those who say fasting does them good, I get headaches. I was on the floor before the Lord. It was a time when the refining fire of the Holy Spirit was working in my own life and rarely have I felt so inadequate for my task as I did during these days. More than ever I could sympathize with Jonah who wanted to run away from his task.

I was flat on my face when Ted Walker walked in, a brother with a pure heart who always encourages me. 'I don't know where to turn anymore,' I told him. We cried out together to the Lord. It was a prayer of desperation, a time when all my own good ideas had to die. Every door had been closed. It seemed the battle was lost. 'Lord,' I said, 'this is your work, not mine.'

That's when God takes us by the hand and says,

'Now child, I'll show you My way.' He does it in a way that we know it has been of His Spirit and not of the flesh.

The phone rang in the apartment. It was a sympathetic official from the Jewish Agency. 'Would you be able to meet a man named David at the Hilton Hotel in Zurich in two days?' He gave no further details, not even the man's surname. He spoke in such secretive terms that I thought it could be a Mossad man I would meet. I sensed it was not a time to ask questions – it was time to act.

I flew to Zurich, where I'd agreed to meet this man in the lobby of the Hilton Hotel. I walked in ahead of the scheduled time. There were a number of people milling about, but my eyes were drawn to a man sitting in the far corner and instantly I knew it was my contact. He turned out to be an Israeli businessman who wanted a ship for import/export business with the Soviet Union.

We talked about a partnership for some time, so much so that David missed his plane to Geneva. Another Israeli businessman turned up and gave him a lift on his private jet, but the next day David was forced to return to Zurich to find a seat on a flight to Tel Aviv. He was astonished to find himself sitting directly behind me on the airplane. 'There are certain things happening here that are not natural!' he exclaimed. We resumed our discussions.

David represented a powerful business consortium, and back in Israel doors suddenly flew open at every level. Talks began with shipping companies and port authorities. We gained strong support in the Knesset

(Israeli parliament) from Michael Kleiner, chairman of the *aliyah* committee. 'I will be your umbrella,' he told me. 'I myself came to Israel by ship back in 1951.' He wrote to us that he was 'deeply touched by the generous donations from Christians around the world.' To help us negotiate with the government of the Soviet Union, we also won the cooperation of the prime minister's Liaison Bureau, which had maintained relations with Soviet Jewry during the years this was officially forbidden.

'We have a vision to carry 25,000 Jews back to their homeland,' I had the boldness to tell these government officials. I estimated it would require a budget of $10,000,000 to $12,000,000. All the gold and silver belongs to my Father, and my faith was growing that He would see that all the funds needed were available on time.

From the beginning we focused on the port of Odessa as the best-situated gateway from the Soviet Union. It would allow for a direct sea route, without the crossing of any international borders. In his vision Steve had seen Jews coming out across Europe and boarding ships in Holland, and some believers along this route had made preparations. Both Steve and I felt this route might be used during a later and greater stage of the exodus – but with the flights and now the shipping I was obedient to what the Lord was showing me.

The time had come to go to the Greek port of Piraeus, where much of eastern Mediterranean shipping is based, and look for a ship. It was very much a learning experience. There were times of fasting an evening meal, spending the evening just to be still before the Lord, really seeking the face of God to know what to do. I came close to agreement for a newly-refurbished Greek ferry ship, in many ways very suitable for our purposes, although the cabins were somewhat smaller than I would have liked and had shared toilet facilities.

'I admit that I still feel that we have not yet got the right ship,' I said in a taped message to our supporters. 'I had hoped to get a real release regarding the ship in my spirit.' But I felt an urgency to press ahead, use the permissions we had been granted, and gain practical experience before signing a long-term contract. At the last minute, however, the owners of the ship telexed to England a withdrawal of their offer, without any explanation. I was back to square one and somehow I had a peace about it. I felt the Lord had intervened and that there would be a better vessel. It was training to wait for His perfect timing.

I returned to Piraeus again, and visited ship after ship. I still remember taking the launch out to the *Mediterranean Sky*. It was a huge ship and the only way on board was up a rope ladder hanging over the side. I clung tightly as the ladder swayed over the choppy water 30 feet below, and finally put a leg up and climbed over the railing onto the deck. It surpassed all the others we had seen, a beautiful vessel with capacity for 900 passengers plus a crew of 120. It was a bigger, better, but also more expensive vessel than I had bargained for. Rex Worth, chief ship engineer with Operation Mobilisation who was accompanying me on this trip, got very excited. 'This is the ship!' he exclaimed.

But I said, 'Lord, I must know from you.' I value counsel and am so grateful for it. But to make critical decisions I need to hear from the Lord myself. To tell the truth I was a bit shocked and surprised at a ship that big. I asked the Lord for a sign. That same day back at the shipping office, He reminded me that the Living Bible renders Isaiah 60:9:

> *'I have reserved the ships of many lands, the very best, to bring the sons of Israel home again from far away, bringing their wealth with them.'*

And I suddenly knew the Lord was saying, 'the best.' I had peace. We reached an oral agreement on chartering the vessel for three trial sailings.

I went to Jerusalem to try to close an agreement on this ship with the business consortium. The Israelis are great bureaucrats. I sat in meeting after meeting. Some went on for six to eight hours. The lawyers were experts in highlighting all that could possibly go wrong. All they managed was to make out of one problem half a dozen problems. Steve as always was ready with a quip: 'It will take a parting of the red tape for this exodus.'

Finally at the end of November we reached an agreement. I was exhausted. What a battle. The terms were not as good as I would have liked, but I believed it had the Lord's approval. We agreed to meet after the weekend to exchange contracts.

But when I turned up three of the four consortium members had cold feet. 'Gustav, we need to postpone,'

one told me. 'We would like you to postpone by a few months.'

I had doubts in my spirit about waiting. I felt we had to go ahead. I told them I needed 48 hours. I wanted to enquire of the Lord. I made half a dozen phone calls all over the world to trusted intercessors who were identifying with us and said, 'This is the position, should we sail now or should we postpone?'

I phoned so many and nobody phoned back. Nobody! I waited all day for an answer. I was under such pressure. It was ten o'clock at night when Ted turned up again to encourage me. As I was sharing my dilemma the phone started to ring, and within one hour all six from all over the world rang, one after the other, and said, 'Gustav, now is the time. Hallelujah.'

Reluctantly the consortium members agreed, and I returned to Piraeus to sign for the ship. But once there a phone call came from our lawyer in Jerusalem. 'Gustav, you cannot sign,' he said emphatically. 'Things are not ripened. The consortium cannot provide services. The entire deal is cancelled or postponed for an indefinite period.' I had to pack my suitcase and return to England. I was devastated.

As I got to my office in Bournemouth the phone rang, and a man who was helping us to gather the Jews in Odessa said in desperation, 'Gustav, we have 500 registered to sail. Some of them have already arrived. They have given up their home, their jobs. You must sail!' What a situation to be in.

As I listened for the leading of the Lord, there came a clear inner conviction: 'Yes, you go now.' I just knew the Lord wanted us to move ahead.

I returned to Jerusalem, where to my surprise most of the consortium members were still ready to work with us and we came to terms on a revised contract. It was then time to finalize our agreement with the owner of the *Mediterranean Sky*. I rang Steve in Seattle and said, 'Steve, this is so big. I need your help.' I was so grateful that he agreed to come with me to Piraeus to sign the contract.

And so we went back to the posh, enormous office of the ship owner, beautifully filled with paintings and models of seagoing vessels. You knew you were in the office of a wealthy tycoon. Steve and I sat at the table with him and the manager of his company and over a meal discussed amendments to the contract. The negotiations became intense. 'I'm not going to do anything!' the manager shouted at one point, and stormed out of the room.

It seemed that everything that could go wrong had. And there is just one thing that stands out in my mind. I was due to sign for three sailings, a commitment for several hundred thousand dollars which Ebenezer didn't have. I would be personally responsible with all that I had as collateral. I sat there looking at this contract and it seemed to me that the figures were getting bigger and bigger. My faith was wavering, and I was thinking, 'Lord, what should I do?' I was perplexed.

Steve started weeping next to me. Later he told me that after so many setbacks he was thinking, 'Lord, is this the end? Should we just get up and walk away from this table?' He didn't speak, he was just crying and crying.

And as I sat there a peace came over me. I knew what I had to do.

I said, 'I will sign.'

And as I signed, Steve jumped up and shouted, 'Hallelujah! Hallelujah!'

'What is happening now?' I asked.

And then he said, 'Gustav, can't you see all the angels? This room is full of angels and they are all applauding that we have signed this contract. It will be recorded in heavenly journals.'

I didn't see the angels. But I had such joy, such a release in my spirit. I put my hand on the contract and said, 'Now we are going to pray that the Lord will watch over, protect, and bless this shipping operation.'

The shipping tycoon, an imposing figure with aristocratic features, was watching all this. I am sure he had never experienced anything like it before. He took out his pen and made the sign of the cross on top of the contract. Operation Exodus was born!

Chapter 4

'Are You not the One who dried up the sea,
The waters of the great deep;
That made the depths of the sea a road
For the redeemed to cross over?
So the redeemed of the LORD *shall return,*
And come to Zion with singing,
With everlasting joy on their heads.
They shall obtain joy and gladness,
And sorrow and sighing shall flee away.'

(Isaiah 51:10–11)

Only two weeks remained between the signing and the first of three sailings of the *Mediterranean Sky*. But before Elsa and I rushed off to coordinate preparations in Odessa, we met with some of the growing number of intercessors who were part of this operation. We knew we were in for a battle, and wanted to make them aware of the significance of this undertaking: opening the first holy highway from the Soviet Union to Israel.

Years before the Lord had sent a remarkable man to teach Elsa and me that intercession was at the heart of our calling to help the Jews home. A letter came from a staff member of the Bible College of Wales inviting me to come and speak about the return of the Jews. I had no desire to go. I felt inadequate to go and speak at a school of the standing of the Bible College of Wales. It had been raised up from nothing 50 years before by Rees Howells, the Welsh coal miner who gave himself to the Holy Spirit and went on to shake the Church with his intercession.

I groped for an excuse. 'Please write and tell them that the date is not convenient,' I told Beverley.

A second letter came offering an alternative date. I couldn't make up my mind. But when I went to an 'Israel Day' sponsored by Prayer for Israel, and greeted the ministry's founder Ken Burnett, he said just one thing:

'When are you going to visit the Bible College of Wales?'

The visit turned out to be one of the great blessings of my life. The college's little meeting hall was packed that evening, and when I finished speaking Samuel Howells, son of Rees Howells, came up. 'We have prayed for the return of the Jews to the Promised Land for many, many years,' he said.

Our guest room that night was opposite the room of Dr Kingsley Priddy, headmaster of the grammar school attached to the Bible College. He was a medical doctor who had prepared to serve the Lord in Africa, but was surprised instead by His call to assist Rees Howells at the college. He was quite an imposing man, an English gentleman, but with a kind face and clear blue eyes that seemed almost to look through you.

As we were talking he mentioned that he had a niece on the south coast of England near our home. 'If you'd ever like to combine a trip to see her with an overnight in Bournemouth, you'd be a most welcome guest,' I told him.

Many visits followed. Kingsley adopted us as his family and we spent precious evenings together. He had countless stories to tell from his life and from the days with Rees Howells, who gave up his money, his food, his reputation – even risked his life – to successfully intercede for others. Kingsley stood with Rees during the war years, as the little band at the college believed the Holy Spirit was bending world events through their prayers.

Kingsley helped us see that our role in the ingathering was like that of Daniel 2,500 years before (see Daniel 9). Daniel understood from reading the book of Jeremiah that the time had come for the Jews to return from their limited exile in Babylon. He stood in their place, identified with them, and allowed the Holy Spirit to intercede through him to accomplish what God had purposed to do.

✣ ✣ ✣

Sunday, December 15th, 1991 is a day which is printed deep in my heart. We took leave from our fellowship, packed, and talked to our children over the phone. Elsa and I were leaving the following morning at 4:00 a.m. for the Ukraine. At 10:30 that night the phone rang. It was one of the Israeli lawyers.

'Gustav, the permit you have for your shipping line qualifies you to carry tourists and freight, but it does not qualify you to carry immigrants. We need an endorsement. You **must** delay.' He was terrified that we would arrive in Odessa and not be able to take one Jew with us. Our operation would become a laughing-stock.

I stood there a minute, phone in hand, and pondered the situation. Our volunteers had started gathering in Piraeus. The shipping company had assembled the crew. The Jews had started to arrive in Odessa. And I had a sense the Lord had given the green light.

'No, we will sail,' I told him.

The lawyer's voice came back over the line. 'It's on your shoulders, Gustav.'

I alerted the intercessors. But that night I didn't sleep much.

In the morning we flew to Kiev, and a lovely Christian girl picked us up at the airport to take us to the station for a train to Odessa. She was working with the Exobus project, bussing *olim* to meet Jewish Agency flights. We had hardly left the airport when we were stopped by a policeman. He came to the window of the car and began speaking rapidly in Russian.

'What does he want? What is he saying?' I asked our escort.

'He wants some money or something,' she said. 'He says we've been speeding.'

'In this old car, and the road in this condition? It's impossible to speed!' I exclaimed.

She handed the officer a pair of nylon stockings through the window. To my amazement he pocketed them and walked off. She explained this was a common way for the police to increase their meagre income. 'We often take something with us when we go out, so we can move on quickly when we're stopped.'

It was the first sign of the chaotic conditions we found facing us. Elsa and I checked into the Londonskaya hotel in Odessa, an aristocratic building with imposing corridors and stained glass windows. It was considered the city's best hotel, but for several days we had no heating and for two days we had no water. The windows were uninsulated and our huge room was an icebox.

As there was no dining room we joined the city residents in the daily search for food, and felt with our own stomachs the still-devastating effect of the famine and economic collapse which had struck the land. Walking down the frozen streets, we passed food shop windows decorated with curtains and lights – but they were empty. One of the largest markets had nothing but dusty bottles of a pickled vegetable and a few wrinkled apples that were rotting away. At home they would only have gone in the rubbish bin.

Great crowds converged on shops where it was possible to buy one of two staples: bread, and vodka, the narcotic in which many drowned their problems. Elsa would queue up for half an hour to purchase a loaf of bread, which we would eat with cheese or a sausage in our room. But food did not seem important to us. We felt privileged to be there. These were historic days.

The ship was on its way, but with three days to go we were still without the right papers. I learned what pressure means. It was a nightmare to see hundreds of Jews gathering with their families and baggage – having left behind their jobs and homes – and not knowing if we would be able to take them.

We were trying to do something during the last dying days of the Soviet Union. The giant had been brought to its knees. The republics had declared their independence and Gorbachev, unwilling to use force against them, was now a powerless figurehead. Already in many cities the statues of Lenin encircled by the intercessors years before were coming down. As we sought permission for our operation we would talk one day with one group, and the next day they were not even in power. The only way we knew to deal with it was on our knees, down on the wooden floor of the frigid hotel room. Elsa and I cried out to the Lord.

Then two men showed up at the port in suits and ties – consuls sent from the Israeli embassy in Moscow. They helped in sensitive negotiations. We received the permission to board *olim* from the port authorities 36 hours before the sailing. It was such a victory – 36 hours before the sailing! Until that time we didn't know whether or not the Jews would be able to board the ship.

The Jews were spread over the whole terminal building with their mountains of luggage, sleeping on their bags for up to three nights while waiting to go through customs. It was drafty and it was cold, but they did not grumble. Their resilience greatly impressed me.

Many had struggled to make it to Odessa from all over the Soviet Union: 55 airports were closed within the former Soviet Union because of a shortage of petrol. We booked a charter flight to bring a group of 98 out of Baku. We had the plane but we just couldn't get the fuel. They decided instead to come by train for the third sailing. We had another group booked from Moldava, but were prevented from sending buses for them by armed conflict in the region.

Everybody had tried to cash in on the *olim* as they made the journey to Odessa – whether the train conductor, the porter, the taxi driver. They all had stories of exorbitant prices and broken promises along the trek from their homes to the port. 'Someone wanted to warm his hands on our grief,' said Nahum, a sculptor, quoting a Russian proverb.

So when they realized who we were and why we were there, they warmly embraced us. There is a special bond in time of crisis. We were their link to the outside world. We had brought hope to their lives.

We tried to bring them refreshments. But each time we gave them mineral water they would open their luggage and offer us in return one of their precious bottles of vodka. '*Spaseeba, spaseeba,*' they thanked us, and motioned for us to sit with them on a piece of their luggage and share some of their smoked fish and bread.

'Why are you going to Israel?' Elsa asked them as they waited. Many said they were fleeing the effects of Chernobyl. Elsa confessed to me that at first she was disappointed this was their reason. 'I expected them to go because they are Jews,' she told me. 'I said, "Lord, I can't believe that they don't understand why they are going at all!"'

Then she saw a bride in a long traditional white gown walking through the port building with her groom on their way to a wedding reception, and was reminded of Revelation 19:7–9. She felt the Lord said, 'That's right, they don't understand, but they're going back for a wedding, the marriage of the Lamb of God.'

There were mountains of luggage at the port, thousands of pieces. The Jews in the land of the north had few suitcases, so they brought their things in cartons, in bags, even in curtains tied up with string. It was so moving to see. There were television sets, carpets – it seemed to me that each one took full advantage of the 500 kilogram luggage allowance. Some of it was rubbish, but they were so attached to it. That was one of the reasons we wanted to bring them home by ship, so they could truly take their belongings with them. It would make their start in Israel so much easier.

But as yet one obstacle loomed between the *olim* and their new life: the customs hall. They were all frightened to go through customs, and Elsa and I soon saw why.

Communism was dying in name only. The hardness of pharaoh's heart was still reflected in the cruel system and hard faces of many of the customs personnel. Every single item was opened as the officials methodically and without compromise carried out their instructions. Every page of every book was checked for hidden banknotes. All this took hours for each family.

Those leaving were regarded as traitors to their country, and treated as such. They were not allowed to take out anything of real value. I saw a woman whose little son had asthma; his medicine was taken away. An 18-year-old girl came crying to me with her mother. 'Could you take for me a little sewing machine?' she sobbed. I couldn't – it would risk the authorities closing us down completely.

Customs officers took jewelry away, sometimes forcibly – the flesh of one woman's finger was torn when a tight-fitting gold ring was forced from her hand. 'Jews go out with all the best things,' the officer told her. 'This is why the Soviet Union is poor.' Another woman sobbed hysterically all the way to the ship after her grandmother's heirloom wedding ring was taken from her.

A middle-aged artist was even denied permission to take out her own paintings on the grounds that 'a work of art is a national treasure.' She too wept as her life's work was taken away. Like many she was uncertain at that moment that she was doing the right thing. I put a hand gently on her shoulder. 'Life is more than material things,' I said through an interpreter. 'You have followed the God of Israel and He will bless you for it.'

What they didn't leave behind was their education. When I first met the mayor of Odessa, himself Jewish, he brought a truthful accusation against us: 'You're taking some of my finest people.' Many of the Soviet Jews were highly-trained engineers, doctors, or musicians.

The story went around at Ben Gurion airport that a man asked the porter, 'I see almost everyone has a violin case or a guitar or something, but there are a few who have no musical instruments. What are they doing?'

The porter turned round and said, 'That is very simply explained – they are the pianists.'

Sailing day finally arrived. Elsa and I rose before dawn and made our way down the great staircase in the biting winter wind and heavy fog. There was the *Mediterranean Sky*!

It was an awesome sight. The ship was brightly-lit, four decks glowing in vibrant gold, orange and white, stretching over 160 metres. It was by far the largest vessel we had seen in the port of Odessa since our arrival. It seemed like a visitor from another world in the drab port. After all the tensions and immense pressure of the days gone by, I couldn't help but some tears ran down my face, tears of joy and tears of relief.

Steve was on board with 20 volunteers. As the ship came in they sounded a ram's horn known as a *shofar*, blown by Jews since the time of Moses as a call of liberation. *Olim* leapt up from the piles of luggage they'd been guarding through the night and ran out of the building shouting and waving.

'How great You are, O God,' my heart sang as I thought of Psalm 147, 'How majestic You are, because what You have proposed, that which is written, You fulfil. You gather together the outcasts of Israel. You heal the broken-hearted and bind up their wounds.'

We really saw a great gathering boarding the ship – 550 in all – the old and the young, the woman with child, the lame and the blind. It was just how Jeremiah 31 described it. They came up the ramp to the ship with their dogs, with their cats, with their birds in cages. We witnessed many moving goodbyes, and saw tears as the Soviet Jews took leave of the only land they'd ever known.

The *Mediterranean Sky* pulled away after midnight. What a wonderful sight to see it float out of the harbour with all the lights. It was finally done. Christians had opened the sea route for Jews from the Soviet Union to Israel!

Two days later Elsa and I celebrated Christmas on our own in Odessa. At 7:00 o'clock that evening Gorbachev appeared on television. 'I hereby discontinue my activities at the post of president of the Union of Soviet Socialist Republics,' he announced, and with him disappeared the Soviet Union. That night the red flag was lowered from the Kremlin. It was six years to the week since the proclamation of the intercessors outside his office.

The *Mediterranean Sky* was crossing 1,150 nautical miles in close to gale force weather. Finally on the fourth morning the storm lifted and the port city of Haifa came in sight, bathed in golden sun. The captain sounded the booming foghorn and police boats rushed out to greet the ship with lights and sirens. *Olim* leaned over the railing, looking at their Promised Land. No one knew whether to laugh or cry.

News reports of the voyage had been suppressed by the Israeli military censor, for concern that the vessel could be the target of a terrorist attack. That same week at the Jewish Agency transit camp in Budapest a car bomb just missed a bus full of *olim* and killed an escorting policeman. But in the morning Israel Radio broadcast the news of the ship's arrival and a crowd of journalists and well-wishers stood waiting on shore.

There was applause, cheering, the playing of a band, and the sound of rubber squeaking against rubber as the boat lodged against the dock. Cameras flashed as those on shore leaned back to photograph the ship towering above them. Minister of Absorption Yitzhak Peretz, himself an orthodox rabbi, could not hide his excitement as he came on board to greet the *olim*. 'You have arrived home, to your family, to your home,' he told them. 'The government of Israel will do all that is possible to help you in your new home.'

He kissed a nine-year-old boy named Genia, whose father introduced the rest of the family and said, 'We are happy that we have arrived to Israel. We waited very long for this moment.'

'When I saw the coast of Israel from the ship I was so excited that I couldn't speak,' added Sophia, an English teacher from the republic of Georgia. 'I believe that it will be good here. It has to be good.'

One of the first *olim* to step off the ship was still clutching his maroon Soviet passport, together with the dark blue Israeli immigration book he'd received from officials on board the ship. 'Shalom, shalom,' he said excitedly.

'I can't tell you what this means,' said an Israeli on the dock who'd helped to gather the *olim* in Odessa. 'I lost my whole family in Europe. If there had been more ships like this, it would have been a different story.'

'Ship brings Jews in new exodus' read the headline on the AP story which appeared in newspapers around the world. The arrival was on the front page of all the major Israeli newspapers, and brought back bittersweet memories for many. In the 1930s and 40s, nearly every Jewish newcomer arrived via the Mediterranean. The best-known ship, the *Exodus*, was intercepted in 1947 by British forces attempting to enforce strict immigration quotas. Three Jewish passengers were killed by British fire and some 100 wounded.

Now we had opportunity to instead publicly stand with the homecoming of the Jewish people. 'These are Christians that love Israel,' our lawyer explained to an interviewer for the national television news. 'They see the significance of the return of the people to the land.'

Johannes and Kjell were also there at Haifa to welcome Steve. 'Both Kjell and I wept when we saw the ship coming in,' Johannes said later. 'It was the most moving experience of all my time as an intercessor. Looking back at what we did on the stairs in Odessa six years earlier, and seeing all these Jews and the enormous mountain of luggage – to realize that God really did honour what we did, that little group.

I didn't even have faith for it when we were there. I felt it was insane what we did. But we were on to a prophetic act of God.

'Incredible. Everything we did came to pass. Everything.'

Chapter 5

'I have chosen you and have not cast you away.'

(Isaiah 41:9)

I was just astounded when the telex from our attorney came in after the docking in Haifa:

'Dear Gustav,

We have just had a most serious complaint from the Ministry of Absorption which not only threatens to abort our whole operation, but can lead to extremely unpleasant and far-reaching consequences.

Some of the Israeli officials on board complained that they witnessed what certainly amounts to missionary activity. On many occasions several of the immigrants were invited to visit and contact the Christians in Jerusalem.'

I had never given any serious thought to the matter. Our guidelines to the team had been clear. We didn't try to preach to the *olim*. We just loved them. The Lord had shown me that we were simply to show them love in action and do our best to help bring them back. I had put this in writing for the

Israeli government. If we broke our commitment, they would bring the line to a halt and we would have failed in what God had called us to carry out.

The *Mediterranean Sky* was returning to Odessa for the second sailing, and the Absorption Ministry demanded that all volunteers be confined to their cabins until they could be removed in Haifa. I went on board the ship when it arrived back in Odessa and gathered the volunteers in a lounge.

'All who are willing to honour our commitment,' I told them, 'I want you to stand to your feet now. We will not be missionaries by words, but we want to be ambassadors by our actions. Each one of you make this declaration before the Lord. If not, get off the ship now.'

All stood to their feet. That gave me confidence that I had a team I could trust, and enabled me to take a clear stand on the issue in the face of government pressure.

Certainly the charge showed some misunderstanding of our motives. But it's equally important that we understand the mind of the Jewish people on this point. For millennia they have resisted efforts aimed at their elimination. Not a few heroically chose death rather than deny the faith of their fathers. The apocryphal books of the Maccabees record the stirring story of the fight against assimilation in the second century BC which preserved Israel and made possible the subsequent birth of the Messiah.

My own children – of Swiss parents but born in Great Britain – are already more British than Swiss. But the Jews have survived as a distinct people while scattered among the nations for nearly 2,000 years. It is nothing less than the hand of God, who promised in Jeremiah 31:36 that the sun and the moon would depart before *'the seed of Israel shall also cease from being a nation before Me forever.'* Jews feel deeply – and rightly – that it is evil to attempt to turn a Jew into a non-Jew.

And in the minds of a majority of the Jewish people **to believe in Jesus is to become a non-Jew.**

> *'The stone that the builders rejected*
> *Has become the chief cornerstone.'*   (Psalm 118:22)
>
> *'Hardening in part has happened to Israel until the fullness of the Gentiles has come in.'*
>
> (Romans 11:25)

This explains the emotional vulnerability of the Israelis to rumours that we were 'missionising'. In their minds arose the horrifying image of these precious *olim* buttonholed in their cabins by zealous Christians urging them to convert and stop being Jews!

Only in recent decades have growing numbers of Jews – like Steve Lightle – recaptured the historical and biblical truth that Jesus and His first followers were practising Jews who upheld the *Torah*, and that faith in Jesus as Messiah can be expressed without leaving the Jewish people. How ironic to the reader of the New Testament book of Acts, who knows that the debate raging among the earliest followers of Jesus was whether Gentiles could believe without first becoming Jews!

In fact we came under attack on this issue from believers as well. It's been painful. A lovely young couple, both Jewish believers in Messiah, came to our hotel room in Odessa. They wanted to come to the port to speak to the *olim*, and couldn't accept our position. But Elsa and I take comfort from the word of God. Ezekiel 36 clearly states that after the Lord brings back His people He will then sprinkle them with water and give them a new heart and new spirit. And just as the first exodus led to the giving of the law, Jeremiah 31 links the final exodus with the making of a new covenant with the house of Israel.

Meanwhile something **was** being communicated to the *olim* and Israeli officials as the volunteers remained on board for the second sailing. It began as our team in Odessa made trip after trip up the ramp to the ship, helping the immigrants with their heavy baggage. They served drinks to the *olim* as they boarded, taught them elementary Hebrew and Israeli songs – even tore up sheets for the infants after the Odessa customs officials went so far as to confiscate all disposable diapers!

Then the night before docking in Haifa, the volunteers held a shipboard celebration for the *olim*. Carol Cantrell, a worship leader from Jerusalem, led them in Hebrew songs, many of them from the *Tanakh* (Old Testament). Two Israeli women who were on board left their government group and came and sat at Carol's feet to sing and clap, their faces beaming. In the center of the lounge a dancing circle formed of Christians, Israelis, and *olim* – one of them the woman who had wept over her ring while boarding the ship, now transformed.

'I felt there was a moment when the burden lifted off them and was replaced with joy,' Carol said later. 'It says so clearly in Scripture they'll come back with rejoicing and singing.'

Everyone stood for the singing of the Israeli national anthem *HaTikvah* (The Hope), and Carol finished with *Shalom, chaverim* (Farewell, friends) as the *olim* went out with tear-streaked faces, some trying to communicate the warmth of their feeling by sending kisses across the room to the volunteers.

'In Russia we knew Jewish people have only enemies in the world,' said one. 'We didn't know of any friends.'

'We have never experienced anything like this in our life,' another said in a tearful goodbye.

What a picture of Jewish-Christian reconciliation!

Later that night the six dark-haired Israeli security men filed into the small lounge on the bow of the ship where volunteers were meeting. With a prod from his partners, one spoke up: 'We just want to say *kol hakavod* (literally "all the honour" to you).'

As they left, Steve led the volunteers in prayer: '*Kol hakavod* to you, Lord.'

✣ ✣ ✣

I started to relax as the third sailing date approached. Once again we had over 500 *olim* gathered. As with the previous sailings, the customs hall opened three days before departure. Our shipping agent came to me after the first day. 'Only 70 cleared today,' he said.

'It looks like the customs officials want to teach you a lesson.' He felt they were delaying the procedures so that not all the *olim* would be able to embark on the last sailing.

Elsa and I had planned to join this sailing to Israel. But I felt we were responsible for every Jew who had come to Odessa. 'If all the *olim* are not able to board, you will have to go ahead on your own,' I told her. 'I'll stay behind to arrange a flight or come to some other solution.'

We started to cry to the Lord so that He would make a way. 'Lord, these are your people, this is your operation,' I prayed. 'We need a miracle.' I knew if it went on like this customs clearance would take another six or seven days. And in fact the next day they again cleared only 70 and the third day as well.

So on the day of departure we still had about 300 people to go through customs on one day. That night I didn't sleep well, and at about 3:00 a.m. I had radio contact with Steve on board the ship and shared the situation with him. He woke up the whole team and told them that instead of sleeping they should come on their knees and intercede for all the *olim* to board the sailing.

The phone rang at 3:30 a.m. and it was a sister from England.

'Gustav, I've been trying for hours to get through to you,' she said excitedly. 'The Lord has given me a word for you. I knew I had to pass it on this very night.' She was adamant. 'Would you turn to Zechariah, chapter 4, verses 6 to 7.'

I opened my Bible and read:

> ' "*Not by might, nor by power, but by My Spirit,*" *says the* LORD *of hosts.* "*Who are you, O great mountain? Before Zerubbabel you shall become a plain!*" '

She didn't know what the mountain was. But I knew the moment I heard it that God had spoken. He would level the mountain of customs which exalted itself against Him.

I said to Elsa, 'Please pack my suitcase as well. We will both be on the ship.'

We managed to sleep an hour, then checked out of the hotel early in the morning with all our belongings and went down to the port. The *Mediterranean Sky* was in and Elsa and I boarded.

There was a different atmosphere on this sailing. The Absorption Ministry had sent a team of ultra-orthodox Jews from a yeshiva to investigate the rumours of missionising. Their leader was a self-assured, 25-year-old former immigrant who had been arrested by the KGB at 15 for Zionist activity. 'You can have **nothing** to do with the *olim*,' he told us at the outset. Reporters from Israeli newspapers were also present to report on the tension.

Among the first passengers to come on board was an elderly couple. They had been three or four days in the terminal and were extremely traumatized. It was the Sabbath and the religious Jews could do nothing to help process them. Our volunteers had to come forward. A married couple from our team was standing at the top of the gangplank with hot chocolate. Just behind them one of the orthodox men was watching what they would do.

The husband put his arm around the shoulder of the elderly man, and his wife around the woman, and the expression of love affected the two so much they broke down and sobbed. Our couple just put their arms around them. Suddenly the expression of the orthodox man, who had been quite hostile, changed and softened.

Throughout the day a slow trickle of *olim* cleared customs and boarded the ship. We were scheduled to leave that evening, but late in the afternoon more than 250 were still waiting in the hall. 'A day's delay in port would cost us between twenty and twenty-five thousand dollars,' I told our team. 'We have to sail on time.'

I asked the intercessors on board to pray while Steve and I went to the ship salon to meet with the Israeli consuls and the captain. Anxiety was written on the faces of all in the room as I laid out for them the situation. Then Eliyahu Ben Haim, the leader of the intercessors, came to the door and called me outside. 'We've had a clear word from Ezekiel 39:28,' he said. 'None of them will be left behind.'

I received it immediately. Money considerations went out – I knew it was the Lord. I returned to the officials.

'This is what the Lord said,' I told them, opening the Bible. 'He will leave none of them behind. We will wait until all are on board.'

As we wrestled against opposition we were learning to proclaim the promises of God from the Scriptures for the Jewish people and the *aliyah*. *'Is not my word like a fire?'* says the Lord in Jeremiah 23:29, *'and like a hammer that breaks the rock in pieces?'*

We realized many in the terminal would not board the ship that night, and had spent hours or even days waiting with little food. The ship's staff graciously prepared a fish dinner and our volunteers set up tables right in the building. All were able to eat well that night. The captain said later he was proud to be part of what was written in the Bible!

We had to delay the ship by 27 hours. In the end they needed the port for another vessel and kicked us out. But every single person was on board, with all their luggage. And I praised the Lord for it. We stood our ground and God gained a tremendous victory, establishing in the heavenlies that nothing could hold back even one of the *olim*.

✢ ✢ ✢

Elsa and I were utterly exhausted. On board ship was the first night in many nights that we really had a good sleep. It felt like paradise after the battle we'd been through every day, every hour in Odessa. The ship seemed to be a dream: warm bath, fresh food, nice tablecloths – all the things we once took for granted. I thought of Psalm 126:

> *'When the* LORD *brought back the captives to Zion,*
>   *we were like men who dreamed.*
> *Our mouths were filled with laughter,*
>   *our tongues with songs of joy.'*
>   (Psalm 126:1–2 NIV)

We indeed had a sense of deep joy and satisfaction as we stood on deck the next morning and looked at the Black Sea stretching off to the overcast horizon.

But we were soon to be reminded that this had indeed been a black sea for the Jews. Some weeks before I'd heard for the first time the horrifying story of another immigrant ship, the *Struma*, which had passed through these same waters exactly 50 years before us. I went to the archives in Jerusalem to get information and pictures which I shared with our volunteers. And once we knew what had happened, we all felt we had to do something about it on this sailing.

Fleeing the Holocaust in Romania, 769 Jews had set sail in the *Struma*, a tiny, hundred-year-old cattle barge meant only for river navigation. After four days of intermittent engine breakdowns they somehow made it to Istanbul harbour, where they sought permission from the British mandatory authorities to enter Palestine (pre-state Israel).

Instead they became part of one of the saddest chapters of British history. While millions were perishing in the Holocaust during the war years 1939 to 1945, those Jews who tried to escape were denied entry into the 'national home' the British government had promised them just two decades before. The British informed the Turkish authorities that the Jews from the *Struma* would not be admitted to Palestine, and asked that they not be allowed into Turkey either.

The ship languished in the freezing harbour for weeks under unimaginable conditions. The Jews were packed below deck without room even to lie down.

There was only one makeshift toilet and no bathing facilities for 769 people. Women were giving birth on board.

On the ship's 35th day in Istanbul the Nazis convened the Wannsee conference in suburban Berlin to decide upon 'the final solution to the Jewish problem,' no doubt taking into account the indifference of the democracies. Numerous appeals were made by the Jewish Agency during these days on behalf of the *Struma* passengers but Britain still refused to yield. On the 70th day, the Turks towed the ship back into the Black Sea and left the Jews without food, water or fuel. The next morning an explosion was heard and the ship disappeared beneath the water. Only one passenger survived.

A group of our volunteers from Britain resolved to hold an on-board ceremony of memorial and repentance as we passed through the Black Sea. Their desire was to stand before God and seek His forgiveness for their nation's part in the tragedy, and ask the Jews for their forgiveness. But the orthodox Jews on board did not want any *olim* to participate in the ceremony. They were very agitated and restless, debating loudly in their cabins until 3 a.m. the night before. We chose not to argue. We were there to serve them.

We came together for the ceremony on the rear of the ship with only the Israeli reporters, photographers, and government officials witnessing the scene. Drops of rain wet the faces of a dozen British believers as they stood in a semi-circle in the freezing Black Sea wind. Fred Wright, a minister from Colchester, spoke in a choked voice. 'We from England are standing here to request forgiveness for the hardheartedness and lack of compassion that our country showed to the passengers of the *Struma*. This was a sinful act, and we humbly ask for forgiveness.'

We stood together in silence for two minutes as the waters churned by behind us. The British believers had prepared a huge wreath – as tall as they were – from flowers and pine branches broken down the previous week by a rare snowstorm in Jerusalem. Two of them carried it to the railing and tossed it into the sea. There was a long, solemn sounding of the ship's horn, as the crew, in dress uniform, saluted the ship's flag which flew at half staff.

It was so moving. Many were crying. The Israelis became part of the ceremony. Several with tear-streaked faces found themselves quite spontaneously embracing the British Christians. 'If you believe and love us this way, it gives us hope for the future,' one said.

Veteran journalist Aviezer Golan, a writer for Israel's leading daily, served as a volunteer in the British army at the time of the sinking of the *Struma*. 'I was the least emotional of the lot,' he said afterwards, 'and I felt very moved. Definitely there was a feeling of coming closer.' He opened his published report on the sailing with a vivid description of the scene.

'It was about eternal and spiritual issues,' explained Bob Hobbs, pastor of an English house church. 'We wanted to settle this and show our hearts. We believe that something happened there that was important to God, and important to the relationship between Israel and England in some way.'

'There was a time for both of us when Israel was just a nation,' added his wife Delphine, 'when my attitude to them was just like any other nation. Even as a born-again believer I didn't have understanding of His glorious purposes for Israel. Progressively He gave me understanding. He began to open His heart to me and touch mine. Now Israel is a very special place for me, and I have a real love for the Jews in my heart. My understanding of the Scripture – *Tanakh* and New Testament – has dramatically changed. So now I am very much allied with Israel, with the homecoming of the Jews, and God's purpose with them until Messiah returns.'

England is not the only nation which turned its back on the Jews. In 1938 the Evian conference was held. Thirty-two nations gathered to discuss the plight of the Jews. Before the conference Hitler threw out to them a challenge:

> 'I can only hope and expect that the other world, which has such deep sympathy for these criminals, will at least be generous enough to convert this sympathy into practical aid. We, on our part, are ready to put all these criminals at the disposal of these countries, for all I care, even on luxury ships.'

One nation after another washed its hands and made the Holocaust possible. The United States set the tone by pledging only to honour its existing miniscule quotas. Less than a year later in a widely-publicized incident the American government refused to accept a boatload of 1100 German Jewish refugees.

They were forced back to Europe where few survived the war. My own people, the Swiss, who took in many thousands of Jewish refugees in the war, closed their borders to an equal number who tried to escape from the Third Reich. They were pushed back over borders for a one-way journey to a concentration camp.

I believe there will not be one reading this whose home country has not done harm to the Jewish people in some way. Many of us have repented; but in my understanding this is only the first step. The Lord has clearly shown us in His word that we should carry the Jews back home to Israel. What an opportunity we have to say to the nation of Israel how deeply we care and so turn past curses into blessings.

Chapter 6

'Deliver those who are drawn toward death,
And hold back those stumbling
to the slaughter.'

(Proverbs 24:11)

'Now I know,' I began to think to myself after the first three sailings. 'I have served my apprenticeship.' It gave me security. Shipping had been new to me, but now I felt more confident.

Later in the year I had a prompting in my spirit that it was time to renew the sailings on a regular basis. I had a sense that we should go with a vessel from a Russian company. The Black Sea Shipping Company (BLASCO) was at the time the biggest, I believe, in all the world. They had 250 vessels. But when I told a shipping man that I wanted to charter with BLASCO, he dismissed it with a wave of his hand. 'BLASCO sends no ships to Israeli waters,' he said. 'Even tourists must change ships in Cyprus.' The president of the Black Sea Shipping Company, I learned, had no love for God's chosen people. He supported the former Soviet policy of boycotting the Jewish state.

So I went before the God of Israel and poured my heart out. I told him, 'This is not right.' And the Lord brought to my mind a word which King David pronounced many years ago over one of his enemies: *'Let his days be few, and let another take his office'* (Psalm 109:8). This was indeed a good word.

I went to the office of my shipping agent in Odessa. 'I want to send a telex to my office in England,' I told him, and sat at his desk and wrote:

> 'Let Christians around the world join me in prayer that Psalm 109:8 will apply to the president of BLASCO and he will be removed.'

I pushed this across the desk to the shipping agent, a young Ukrainian professional dressed in suit and tie. He looked at it and was astounded.

'Are you sure?' he asked. 'It is not wise what you are doing.'

I understood him. There is never a sense of complete freedom in the former Soviet Union; people watch their speech far more carefully than we in the West. Sometimes associates would ask me to walk with them outside to discuss confidential matters. And the president of BLASCO was a powerful man in the Ukraine.

'I am sure,' I said nonetheless. I felt the Lord had given the release to do it.

Three days later Elsa and I were packing our suitcase at the hotel when I heard a knock on our door. I opened it to find the shipping agent. He looked at me and said, 'What kind of a man are you?'

'Why? What has happened?'

'This morning the news came on the radio – the president of the Black Sea Shipping Company is under investigation for corruption.'

The president was removed, and his replacement was willing to work with us. We serve a great God!

Next came the challenge of finding a partner to handle the operation in Israel. I had quite hard discussions about this in January 1993 with shipping company owner Moshe Mano. We were miles apart following one long night in a lawyer's office in Tel Aviv.

Moshe offered to drive me to the central bus station so I could catch the midnight bus back to Jerusalem. He lost his way, and at a traffic light rolled down his window to ask directions from the next car. But instead he got excited, parked the car and jumped out. He talked very intently with the other driver for several minutes as I sat looking at my watch. I must admit that I got a bit irritated, thinking I would miss the last bus. Finally he came back to the car.

'I've been trying to reach that man for several days,' he told me. 'His only son Ronen was shot in Hebron a month ago while on guard duty. There's a bullet still lodged in his brain.'

Moshe paused and looked over at me. 'You know, money is not that important,' he said. 'Life is important.'

We both knew that night there'd be no problem reaching an agreement. And in fact together we chartered the 500-bed BLASCO passenger ship *Dmitry Shostakovich* for 25 weekly sailings between April and

September 1993. It was a beautiful ship, built in 1980 at the Polish shipyard of Lech Walensa.

After long negotiations we also leased a former Communist youth camp in Odessa to house and feed the *olim* for several days before each sailing. Elsa and I moved in to coordinate the operation in mid-March as the grounds were still covered with snow. Volunteers began streaming in from many nations of the world to serve with us.

At first we found the camp was a dark place. Strange characters went in and out of the hotel. We heard dogs barking all night, and saw them limping about in the day as if they'd been beaten. The weather was freezing and the heating and hot water were often out of order. Most of the toilet seats were missing from the bathrooms. The food was awful. And unless a translator was with us the language barrier left us helpless.

The staff looked at us with cold suspicion. 'There's not much willingness to please,' Elsa commented to me after a few days. 'It's more like negotiating our rights.' I had to agree. The staff carried out their duties with empty, hard expressions, projecting their own difficult past. I did meet some Ukrainians during this time who went out of their way to be helpful. But that was certainly the rare exception and not the rule. When I looked into the eyes of the former Soviet people I could hardly ever detect a sparkle and I couldn't help thinking how much they need Jesus.

We found everything was an effort in the post-communist Ukraine. Technologically they were 50 years behind the West. It was easier to drive across town to someone than to reach them by phone. One morning I needed to make photocopies. There were two shops in town. I went to the first and found it had no electricity. I crossed town to the second and found it had no paper.

I took a translator with me and went down to the port. I knew we'd have to come to some terms with the Ukrainian customs officials if we were to avoid the scenes of the earlier sailings. We faced twelve customs and immigration officials across a long table in a frigid room.

I was a bit naive. 'We believe that we will carry as many as 8,000 emigrants on these sailings,' I told them. 'I've come to see what your requirements are.'

There were no smiles. The temperature visibly dropped.

'We are not equipped for emigration,' the lead official replied grimly. 'If you want us to be, you must provide.' They pulled out lists of demands that I estimated would cost hundreds of thousands of dollars: x-ray equipment, computers, and building a storage room.

I declined our lawyer's offer to write to the Ukrainian president about the customs impasse. Instead I turned to the Lord. And after many battles and negotiations to the early hours, we came to terms. Together with our Israeli shipping agent we did indeed agree to purchase x-ray equipment, which would allow customs to process the *olim* without the painstaking opening of every bag. The new procedures would cut a family's waiting time with their possessions from days to 3–4 hours.

But even as one problem was sorted out, another came. No ship insurance was in place. No approval had come from the Ukrainian Foreign Ministry. No wood could be found to crate the baggage. The equipment we had promised the customs officials didn't arrive. Word came from the Absorption Ministry in Israel that the first sailing date was unacceptable, as the ship would arrive just before the start of Passover, when the *Torah* allows no work. 'If it's late we'll leave it at sea with no provisions,' they warned. To top it all there was no fuel in the port for the sailing!

And then – we found that the optimistic reports of the Ukrainian Jewish group responsible for recruiting *olim* were illusory. Only 43 were booked for the first sailing. It seemed all hell had been turned loose against this shipping line. Faith levels began to drop and a few volunteers began to lose heart and question our mission.

I felt that a strong word was needed to silence dissent. The night before we were due to board ship I called the team together. 'We're going to load up with luggage tonight, take it to the port, and put it on the ship,' I told them. 'And it's going to sail because God said it's going to sail.'

The next day, even as Elsa and I were going up the ramp with the last of the *olim*, a barge came up and filled the ship with fuel. On board we found a group of our intercessors. They had stood by us unshakably through this time, disregarding what they were seeing and hearing. I sat across from them at the table but couldn't speak. I just wept with relief. It had a tremendous effect on us all. We embraced, and Elsa and I walked back down the ramp into the gathering darkness.

✤ ✤ ✤

The second sailing was only a week away, and we were dismayed to learn that there were even fewer *olim* registered than for the first. They had flocked to our trial sailings from all over the Soviet Union a year before. Many had been waiting years for the opportunity.

But the torrent of *aliyah* had now dwindled to a steady stream of just one-third the previous year's peak. There were also new border and custom controls which restricted *olim* and their belongings from entering the Ukraine from other republics, and the Jewish Agency had put in place its own structure of direct flights. Instead of more bookings we got cancellations.

We saw that we must develop our own booking network. But as we began to contact the Jewish community, they were slow to respond and were reluctant to display our information. Many of the Jews of the Ukraine still bore open wounds from their terrible suffering at the hands of Gentiles during the Holocaust.

During our first visit to Kiev, the capital of the Ukraine, Elsa and I had visited the grassy park on the outskirts of the city named Babi Yar. A guide told us its story. When the German army came into Kiev in 1941, they announced to all the Jews, 'Get your belongings ready, you are being resettled.'

They were gathered in a huge crowd at Babi Yar. Each family left its money at a table. Their belongings were laid down in a pile. Then they were told to undress and driven in groups of one hundred to the edge of a great ravine. A woman who gave birth at the site went with her newborn baby in her arms. As they approached the ravine the realization came that there would be no resettlement. They were mowed down by machine gun fire. Over 33,000 people died that day. Many were only injured and buried while still alive. Our guide told us that the earth was moving for days after the massacre.

Elsa and I were devastated. We walked silently back to the car. Neither of us could say anything.

We'd heard about this before. But somehow when we really saw with our own eyes – to know it happened **here** – we faced the evil and cruelty of mankind. It was a shock for us to accept, coming from our sheltered background.

Later Elsa and I went to an uncultivated pasture near the port in Odessa. It seemed no one wanted to build on it. A modest memorial stone explained why. In October 1941, six days after German and Rumanian troops had occupied Odessa, an explosion blew up the Rumanian command headquarters and killed the commanding general. As retribution 19,000 Jews were assembled here in a fenced-off lot, sprayed with gasoline and burned alive. The next day 16,000 more were marched in long columns to a nearby village. First they were machine-gunned in groups of 50 and then, to save time, locked in warehouses which were set ablaze. Panicked mothers attempting to throw their children from the windows were met with grenades and bullets.

'Where were you Christians when all this happened?' one Jewish leader asked when we said we'd come to help them go home. 'Nobody came in our time of need.'

This initial suspicion and mistrust was compounded by opposition from a source I'd never expected. Instructions came to Jewish Agency field workers from headquarters in Jerusalem to steer *olim* away from our sailings. Families were warned that if they arrived in Haifa port with their belongings they would be stranded at the dock with no one to help them.

Finally advertisements appeared in the Ukrainian newspapers featuring a picture of a ship with a big red X over it. Underneath was the headline:

'THE SAILINGS FROM ODESSA TO HAIFA
ARE NOT TAKING PLACE.'

It was signed by the Jewish Agency.

I was shattered. I knew when I was going into the former Soviet Union I would have a battle on my hands. I didn't expect it with the Jews or within Israel. But then the Lord graciously reminded me that Moses had his hands full not only with the Egyptians, but with his own people. Nothing had changed.

Initially Agency officials had grave reservations that we Christians would have the ability to do this work. They feared we might disappear after a few months, leaving them to take over our responsibilities. Somehow it seemed they also saw our help as competition in a sphere which had until then been exclusively theirs.

We hit the low point on the fifth weekly sailing, that left Odessa on Good Friday at the end of April. 320 beds were paid for. Only 10 *olim* were on the ship.

I came under severe attack. By now half our volunteers had left or been dismissed. Some men who had worked with us called a public meeting in London to ask me to justify why we were spending so much money for so few people. They doubted the vision and felt that I was unwise to charter such a big ship for weekly sailings.

I felt humiliated by the call for a public meeting. I asked myself where it would lead. Would I be exposed as one who had acted out of the flesh? Had I really heard the Lord? I felt that I had failed, and for the first time began to think of giving up.

In the middle of the night I got out of bed in our room at the Odessa camp and lay on my belly, nose down on the carpet, weeping. 'I can't take it anymore,' I cried out to the Lord.

A breaking up was going on, a breaking of my pride that I was the one chosen to do this work. It was painful, humbling.

I climbed back into bed, sobs still racking my body as I lay next to Elsa. She was awake and spoke to me in the darkened room. 'I want to tell you a story. There was a man who built the best ship ever. It took him 120 years. And there were only eight people on it.' I realized she was talking about Noah. It was an amazing revelation. It gave me courage. Elsa was marvellous at this time. She never doubted one moment that we had been called by the Lord.

A few days later we flew to Jerusalem. The Jewish Agency now made an offer to pay us $180 for each immigrant we brought on our sailings! I was at first overjoyed and thought this might be our answer.

'Lord, what are you saying?' I asked. 'Do we accept or not? Do we continue sailings or not?' Our team in Odessa came out against accepting the offer, but I still took over a week to consider. It offered a way of escape from the criticism which was then reaching a crescendo. But finally the Lord did not allow me to accept. He reminded me that He has called the Gentiles to carry His sons and daughters back home.

The public meeting was held on *Tisha b'Av*, the day of disasters on the Jewish calendar. On this same date Solomon's temple was destroyed by the Babylonians in 587 BC **and** the second temple by the Romans in AD 70. With very mixed emotions of pain, indignation, and apprehension I flew to London with Elsa.

We walked into the meeting room in a hotel near Heathrow airport and found about 50 people there. Several of our faithful intercessors were on hand just to pray. I took a seat at a table at the front with Johannes and Kjell. I saw other leaders of the Intercessory Prayer Conference who had flown in: Eliyahu Ben Haim from Israel and Robert Währer from Switzerland. Kingsley had come in from the Bible College of Wales. These men all knew me intimately and had been standing with us in prayer. All were recognized Christian leaders. Even the dissenters respected and accepted them.

The meeting was quite tense at the beginning. Johannes emerged as the chairman and together with Kjell defused the situation. They handled the discussion in the Spirit and with a sensitive, listening ear. All had the opportunity to speak from the heart. No one was steamrollered.

A few argued that we were wasting God's resources. I was astounded when the leaders completely dismissed the financial issue. 'The number of *olim* is not the issue,' Johannes said. 'We must look at the wider spiritual dimension.'

It became clear that the united opinion of the leadership was that the call we had was from the Lord, and it was His will that the sailings proceed. The leaders affirmed their willingness to share in the responsibility, and from this the Ebenezer Emergency Fund gained its international advisory board. Not all in the end rejoiced, but there was a sense of peace.

We stayed for a meal afterwards with friends. 'Am I glad this is over,' I sighed to Elsa. Only then I started to realize all of this had been from the Lord. It had been one of the most painful episodes of my life, but I saw God meant it for good. I no longer felt so important – this was really God's work and I was just one of His servants. He is in the business of making us into men and women He can use. As Elsa often reminded me, 'It's not what we do for the Lord which really counts, but what He is doing in us.'

Now for the first time I grasped that our prayer and action counted beyond the boundaries of Ebenezer's own operation. I wrote to our supporters:

'Out of these past three months the Lord has moved mightily in the heavenlies, laying the foundations of a work far greater than anyone of us can visualize. The Lord has shown us so clearly the intercessory nature of the project, that we do not just have the privilege of bringing out thousands of *olim*, but through overcoming, at every level, every opposition that hell can bring against the work, the Holy Spirit would gain a position of intercession for Jews worldwide to be brought home to Israel, according to God's word.'

Kingsley's experience with intercession helped bring this into focus for us. He was always keenly interested in our work, and in a remarkable letter helped me also to see why I'd been led by the Holy Spirit to decline the underwriting of the Jewish Agency for Operation Exodus. The true intercessor, he wrote, becomes **personally responsible** for the object of his prayer:

'You see, Intercession is not prayer, nor even very intense prayer. Anyone may pray, and pray earnestly, for something, and yet not be committed to be irrevocably responsible, at any cost, for its fulfilment. The intercessor is.

In Intercession there is Identification with the matter or persons interceded for. The intercessor is willing to take the place of the one prayed for; to let **their** need become **his** need; to let **their** need be met at **his** expense and to let **their** suffering become the travail of **his** own heart.'

That is how the Lord Jesus *"made intercession for the transgressors"* (Isaiah 53:12). *"He was numbered with the transgressors,"* and *"He was wounded for* (their) *transgressions"* (Isaiah 53:5). He had to be "identified" with sinners; He secured their pardon by vicariously paying the debt that they owed.'

(The full text of this letter is reprinted in Appendix 2)

To our surprise the leading Israeli newspaper *Yediot Ahronot* had picked up on the crisis in Odessa. They sent a journalist to investigate, and the same week as the Heathrow meeting published a multi-page spread in their weekend edition exposing what they called the Jewish Agency's efforts to 'torpedo' the sailings.

It was taken up in the Knesset. I was called to testify before a special session of the immigration committee. I came over from Odessa on a sailing the night before. I was sweating. To go to parliament. Somehow I was unable to prepare what to say.

That morning I entered the crowded meeting room and saw a high-powered team from the Jewish Agency, members of Knesset, government officials, and the news media. As the meeting began Yasha Kedmi, who had years of experience with Soviet Jewry as head of the prime minister's Liaison Bureau, came out strongly behind us. He argued that the decision of many *olim* to come to Israel hinged on whether they could bring their possessions with them, which our sailings allowed. He also revealed that since 1989 his bureau had been calling for the opening of sea routes in case of emergencies when flights might be impossible.

I listened to a whispered translation of his comments from Hebrew:

'This group wants to finance the attempt of the state of Israel and of the Jewish people to bring *olim* by way of the sea. So why not agree and tell them, "Thank you"?'

I had given the committee members a paper listing some of the biblical references undergirding our work. Knesset member Avraham Ravitz, an orthodox rabbi with full beard and black clothing, interrupted the meeting to ask for a Hebrew Bible, then turned and addressed me for the first time. 'In your paper you brought a quotation from Jeremiah 16, which is a correct and lovely verse. I want to direct our attention to what is said at the end of the chapter:

"O LORD, my strength and my fortress,
My refuge in the day of affliction,
The Gentiles shall come to You
From the ends of the earth and say,
'Surely our fathers have inherited lies,
Worthlessness and unprofitable things.'
Will a man make gods for himself,
Which are not gods?"   (Jeremiah 16:19–20)

'I will tell you why I raise these verses. On the sailing two years ago – and I don't know if this was your organization – matters were not so smooth from the standpoint of the Christian group's attempt to influence the *olim*. I'm speaking with you in the most open manner, as one religious man to another.

'Truly Jews should be brought to Israel at any price, but not at the price of an attempt to influence them to receive a different religion. I do not agree to this price ... We must remember we are dealing with *olim* who were cut off from the religion of their fathers for 73 years, and they are coming here to return to their roots. And *oy vavoy* to us if they will be influenced by a group of missionaries on their way to the country ... We need to strictly guard the Jews making their way to the Holy Land, to the land of their fathers and to the religion of their fathers, to the land of the *Tanakh* which is promised to them by the Holy One, Blessed be He, so they will not be confused.'

I knew I had to speak up. 'Mr Chairman, I'm surprised to find myself in the Knesset. I'm a simple guy who serves an extraordinary God. And I know that the God of Israel called me to serve and to carry home the children of Israel, the chosen people.

'I want to say in the clearest possible way that my hands are clean and my motives are pure. All of the volunteers working with us pledge that they have no missionary intentions and they will not engage in missionary activity.'

At this point I also pulled out my Bible. 'Listen, this book is written by you. If you read your own Bible it says in Isaiah that the Gentiles should carry your sons and daughters back. I want you to know that all over the world there are Christians who have committed themselves to bringing the Jewish people home.

'During the last two-and-a-half years I spent more

time in Odessa than any other place, and I have travelled extensively throughout the former Soviet Union. And I understand that the situation is deteriorating. We are living on borrowed time. We need to do all that we can to bring these *olim* home as quickly as possible.

'I think it is very important that there will be an additional escape route beyond what is now established. In chapter 60, verse 9 of Isaiah it says explicitly that they will come home by ship, that *"the ships of Tarshish will bring your sons from afar."*

Rabbi Ravitz was following along in his Hebrew Bible. 'And it is also written there,' he interjected, ' *"that their silver and their property is with them."* That is to say, their baggage is with them. Isn't that what we've been talking about here?'

From that point he and the rest of the committee were behind us. And without my speaking a word about the Jewish Agency, that which was covered was revealed and the hidden things made known. 'The Agency was wrong all the way,' Uri Gordon, head of its immigration department, told the committee. He showed them telegrams sent to Agency representatives instructing them to begin helping us.

'We call on the Jewish Agency to settle this matter at the earliest possible time,' concluded the chairman, Emanuel Zisman, at the end of the hearing. 'We recommend that this be given the highest priority ... because you see this involves a real danger of loss of life.'

Afterwards the rabbi came and shook hands with me and said, 'Now I feel more comfortable about your helping our people to come home.' He said I had spoken well. Not me! The Lord had taken me by His hand.

Also Uri Gordon wrote us that week, 'to extend our appreciation to your sponsors. You are part of a great historic event, the ingathering of the Jewish people to their land.'

✢ ✢ ✢

On the Odessa base a new atmosphere was blooming. We rebuilt our team of volunteers, drawing on some 20 nations, and there was real joy among them. They were united in their love for the Lord and His word. Even after tiring hard work they could sing and dance to Him. The *olim* could see them shining with the love of the Lord.

A German couple, Hinrich and his wife Elke, took over the leadership of the team and brought strength and commitment as I was travelling to London and Jerusalem. Hinrich had been managing the construction of a huge power plant when he applied to join us months earlier. Our invitation arrived the day he finished the project. He immediately took a leave of absence to join us.

At the camp he recounted for us a conversation with his employer at the celebration of the plant's completion. 'Why are you going to help the Jews?' he asked Hinrich. 'We know that young girls are romantic and old ladies pray, but why you?'

'God said to Abraham, "I will bless those who bless you,"' Hinrich replied. 'I'm not afraid to ruin my career. You'll promote me while I'm away.' His boss recalled that remark when he phoned Hinrich months later in Odessa with news of a promotion!

Hinrich's father was an officer in the German army and had taken part in the brutal occupation of Odessa. Now as we met with the *olim* in the camp's dining hall for a farewell evening before each sailing, Hinrich read to them the prophecy of Isaiah 60:14:

> *'Also the sons of those who afflicted you shall come bowing to you.'*

And we really embraced the Ukrainians on the camp staff, treating them as human beings, with a smile. It was new for them. Under the communist system, they had worked under fear and the pressure of the boss. Now for the first time each was respected as a person. Gradually we broke the spirit of the camp. A big *babushka* (grandmother) in the kitchen insisted on kissing me whenever she saw me.

We had an evening together with the staff, and gave them Russian Bibles and children's Bibles. Most took the children's Bibles, which were illustrated and easier to understand. 'Look, this is a book written thousands of years ago,' I told them. 'We live in a time when what is written by these men of old, these prophets, is taking place. You are a privileged person to have a part in this.'

One gray-haired man on the staff always looked stone drunk. He came to me the day after our meeting. 'I couldn't drink last night,' he said through a translator. 'I was reading the Bible the whole time.' When we gave them the Bible they treated it with far greater respect than in the West. This was a forbidden book for 70 years. They realized we were putting something very special into their hands.

Then came perhaps the most amazing development of all. Israel's only television channel had sent a crew to Odessa to prepare a documentary on our work. The night that the stunning news first broke of the Rabin-Arafat accord, all Israel gathered before the television screen for the details. Then the newscaster said, 'We have one more report, that belongs perhaps to a different rhythm, that of God – but it too has good news and hope for the future.'

With that the programme switched to strains of our volunteers singing 'He Has Made Me Glad' in the Odessa camp. There followed a remarkable 14 minutes guiding the Israeli people through our whole operation, from picking up *olim* at the railway station to dropping them off at the dock in Haifa. There were interviews with several volunteers, but the focus of the programme was on actions more than words. Before the eyes of the nation passed scenes of service and love: volunteers from all the earth carrying the immigrants' baggage, dancing with their children, waving and singing farewell at dockside. Lingering close-ups searched the volunteers' faces. One could almost hear the questions being asked: Who are these people? Why are they doing this for us?

From the sure death of the Good Friday sailing the Holy Spirit had brought resurrection. Operation Exodus had shown the entire nation God's love and faithfulness to His word.

✤ ✤ ✤

During these weeks the number of *olim* on each sailing had been steadily rising. The name of Ebenezer was becoming well-known and the Jewish community started to accept and trust us. For the 25th and final sailing of the year our volunteers picked up 22 different groups of *olim* at the train station, plus others brought in by bus from outlying villages. The camp was fully booked and we were forced to open a second. We faced a new and welcome crisis: would we have enough beds on board ship?

In the end all were able to embark. Some volunteers slept on cabin floors. 'Tonight my heart is full of thanks,' I told them after Elsa and I boarded. 'God has answered my prayers.'

As we were going under the bridges of Istanbul I was standing near a handicapped immigrant who was using a pair of binoculars. 'May I borrow those for a moment?' I asked him. I wanted to study the old stone fortresses on the shore. He handed them to me, but when I went to return them, he refused.

'No, no – they are yours,' he told me. 'I want you to keep them. You have done so much for my people.' I was deeply moved. They were probably his most prized possession.

The evening before docking in Haifa we savoured more of the sweet aroma of reconciliation as we shared an evening with the *olim*. How they cheered when I told them the story of the removal of the BLASCO president earlier that year!

'We are so used to that attitude,' one woman explained. 'Someone not liking us simply because we are Jews.' They were amazed to think that God would intervene in response to prayer.

'I just want to praise the God of Israel for all His help,' I told them. 'You need to learn to pray yourselves in Israel, and God will help you with your problems.'

The love of God filled the room like a cloud as our volunteers came and shared their hearts with the *olim*. Afterwards I saw an American named Becky exchanging tears and hugs with a greying, bent immigrant named Rebekah. 'We're working together as one,' Rebekah told us. 'I've never felt such personal attention and love.'

An older man who looked like a former officer in the Red Army came to me, shook my hand, and said, 'Once I was a communist. But now I believe in God, seeing the love shown to us by your people.'

Also with us was a Holocaust survivor named Joseph. We had invited him and other survivors to travel on the ship for a once-in-a-lifetime tour of Israel, even though they did not plan on emigrating. 'We are very surprised and totally amazed,' he said after the meeting. 'We were really crying. We couldn't believe it was true.'

He shared with us his story from the war years:

'My family and I, together with all the Jews, were gathered by the Germans. With my mother and sister, my grandfather and brother, we walked 35 kilometres to a camp. It was very cold; many died on the way. The camp was called the "place of death". Those who entered it didn't leave. We

112

lived in terrible conditions. My mother and sister died there.

Before the war we had a Russian woman living and working in our home. She did all the best she could do for us. She followed us to the camp. She tried to pass food to us. After the camp was liberated by the Russian army, she took my older brother and me and helped us to find our father. She was a real Christian, the most precious person I've met in my life. She took the role of saviour in our family. We wouldn't have survived without her.'

For Elsa and me it was like a ray of sunshine to hear from time to time of these Christians who risked their lives to save Jews during the Holocaust. Such help was forbidden by the German occupying forces on pain of death. We remembered others – the Jews called them 'righteous Gentiles' – like Corrie ten Boom, whose family hid Jews in their home in occupied Holland. When arrested she and her sister were taken in a cattle car together with Jews to a concentration camp. Only Corrie survived. These were true intercessors – standing with the Jews even to the point of death.

The director of the Department for the Righteous at the Yad VaShem Holocaust memorial and museum in Jerusalem, Dr Mordecai Paldiel, reported that a majority of the hundreds of rescuers he's studied were motivated by their Christian faith. The Church as an institution came out of the Holocaust besmirched, in his view, by its failure to take a stand. 'But the small persons had a better grasp of what Christianity was than the hierarchy,' he said. 'As a religion of faith, love, and brotherhood, Christianity has shown itself capable of being a very potent force ... The Sermon on the Mount, the Good Samaritan – they were moved by it. It speaks in favour of the teachings of Christianity.'

Chapter 7

' "Hear the word of the LORD, O nations,
And declare it in the isles afar off, and say,
'He who scattered Israel will gather him,
And keep him as a shepherd does his flock.'" '

(Jeremiah 31:10)

We had only just cleared all the bills from the sailings when Esther turned up in my Bournemouth office. I wasn't fooled by her head of white hair. This widow and former headmistress had been a strong and determined volunteer with us through the difficult months in Odessa. And rather than return to England's quiet shores after the last sailing, she and another Englishwoman set off in the thick of winter for the former Soviet republic of Armenia. Esther had heard of severe conditions there and went to investigate the state of the Jewish community.

They met some Armenian Jews, struggling to live with the effects of the massive 1988 earthquake and ongoing warfare with Azerbaijan. Electricity came on for just one or two hours a day, and nobody knew when. Fresh water only came every three days.

'Do you want to go to Israel?' Esther asked a Jewish community leader in the capital city, Yerevan.

'There are no flights to Israel from our country,' he replied. 'The only way is to first go all the way to Moscow, and we don't have the money for that.'

'What if we brought a plane?' Esther persisted. The leader shrugged sceptically.

Esther and her friend promised to return. In England they gathered aid, and flew back into Armenia in February with many boxes of supplies for the Jews. The community was stunned. The women had kept their word. No one had fulfilled promises before.

'Is there **really** any possibility you'd get us on a plane to fly to Israel?' the leader asked.

'Well ... yes,' Esther said, thinking, 'I don't know who will pay!'

Returning to England they went to an aircraft charter company and booked a plane for a London/ Yerevan/Tel Aviv/London circuit three months hence. They had no money. Esther had only a pension. Her friend owned a home. They came out from the charter office and stood on the pavement and looked at each other. 'What have we done?' Esther said. 'We've booked an airplane that will cost £60,000!'

That's when she came to me. 'We know not to collect money for the plane,' Esther said with quiet certainty. She was always sensitive to the instruction of the Holy Spirit. 'We can collect humanitarian aid in England to **bring** on the plane, but God is going to pay for the plane.'

At the end of her report Esther smiled. 'Would you pray about whether Ebenezer should be involved?'

'You know, you're always costing me a lot of money,' I teased her as I thought over our situation.

There had been a period of extensive prayer and waiting before we covered the sailing bills, and I felt no inclination to branch out into a new and unknown republic. 'I would need a clear sign from the Lord to know if we should get involved in this.'

Elsa and I started to pray, and didn't seem to get any answer. Week after week I would get a phone call from Esther, looking for an answer. 'I've heard nothing from the Lord,' I told her. 'This has nothing to do with me.'

I felt for her deeply after my own experiences. But much as I enquired of the Lord about our involvement, there was only silence. I knew I had no choice but to stand still and to continue waiting on Him. 'We know that the Lord God of Israel has the whole situation in hand,' I faxed Esther, who was now organizing the Jews in Yerevan. 'We feel he will make a way of escape and should we receive a direct signal you will, of course, be the first to know.'

Finally, Esther's colleague phoned at 11 a.m. one day and said, 'Unless we pay today the flight will be cancelled, and it will do tremendous harm because we have gathered humanitarian aid and, more importantly, Jews to fly out.' She asked for a loan, and was willing to sell her house to repay it.

'I'll give you my reply by 3 p.m.,' I told her, and called a few trusted intercessors and Elsa and asked them to urgently seek the Lord's guidance. It was in fact Elsa who came back first. She had felt a prompting to look up Scriptures which spoke of lending, and came to Luke 11:5–8, the friend asking to borrow three loaves at midnight.

'They are really desperate,' she told me. 'It is nearly midnight for the flight. And they have been knocking for all these weeks.' The amazing thing is that a Swedish intercessor then faxed me the same words. I knew the Lord was saying it was right – and phoned back to say we'd cover the cost as a three-month loan.

Only later did Elsa share with me the other Scripture she had found: 'When you loan, do not expect to be paid back!'

So I established direct contact with the air company and satisfied myself that we had a proper contract. They were experienced in such mercy flights. I packed my suitcase. I was sure I'd be on the plane. But somehow the Lord didn't give me the green light to go. I had no peace about it. It was disappointing – I could not understand.

On flight day I asked the airline to keep us posted. The first report was all okay, but hours later they called to say they had no landing permission at Ben Gurion airport. 'What do you mean, you have no landing permission?' I questioned. 'You should have applied long before this!'

I soon realized that permission had in fact been denied. The Israeli aviation authorities had checked with the Jewish Agency, which cast doubt on the operation by saying there were few if any Jews in Armenia! I was taken aback. The aircraft was already in the air.

I sent an urgent fax to the Israeli ambassador in Moscow, whose consuls had approved the documents of all these Jews: 'You issued the visas, now permission to enter the country is needed.' No answer was forthcoming. Hours went by.

Esther phoned to tell me the plane had landed and the aid was unloaded. Then the phone line to Armenia went dead. Our efforts to call all afternoon were in vain. I drew up a contingency plan to take the plane into Cyprus and put the *olim* on the overnight ferry to Haifa. Finally about 10 p.m. came the call from the airline confirming, much to my relief, that Israel had granted landing permission. Now I understood that the Lord had kept me back from the flight in order to manage this crisis.

But in Yerevan Esther found that after unloading the plane the authorities wouldn't let it depart. They demanded $9,000 in cash fees rather than the $500 previously agreed. Esther spent the entire day trying to negotiate without success, meeting people, running up and down stairs. There was nothing to eat or drink in the airport. Around midnight the power was out and she was going up the stairs in the dark. She went to a corner and felt as if arrows were coming at her from every direction.

'Have we been two foolish women, Lord?' she cried out. 'Doing something presumptuous, not from you? All these Jews down here with no homes, and no money to pay for the plane. We don't have $9,000 to get them to Israel. What are we going to do?'

She felt as if something like a shaft of light hit her, and all she heard was 'Get the money.' She thought, 'Get the money? Then it must be here somewhere!' and ran back to her friend. They pooled their resources, and turned to a pastor friend. He brought all the money he had, $1,500 given to help buy an office for his church. All together they came up with $3,000.

Esther prayed, 'Lord, where are we going to get the other $6,000 from?' 'Go to the pilots,' came the thought. She and her friend ran over the pitch black airfield to find the plane. There were the pilots and crew, sitting in the dark waiting for news. Esther told them what had happened.

'How much do you need?' the captain asked.

'Six thousand dollars,' she said.

He looked at them in amazement. He put his hand in his pocket and brought out a wad of bills. 'I think you'll find $6,000 here,' he said. 'You can borrow it and pay it back when you can.' As he was getting dressed for the flight the pilot had seen his savings sitting on the cupboard. On impulse he stuffed the money in his pocket. It was the exact amount needed! Many hours later the plane landed at Ben Gurion airport, carrying 67 *olim*.

Esther remained in Yerevan, where she and her partner were praying about the finances to repay Ebenezer for the flight. She told me she saw a picture in her mind of an invoice which said, 'Paid in full.' Minutes later the phone rang. It was my fax, sharing with them the second Scripture Elsa had given. God had released us to pay for the plane.

Esther wasn't finished. A plea came for help from Jews in the neighbouring region of Nagorno-Karabakh, scene of fierce battles between Armenia and Azerbaijan. Esther set off in a private car to investigate with a Czech volunteer named Vlasta.

Bagrat, from the church in Yerevan, was driving. As they climbed the serpentine road into the mountains snow began to fall, more heavily the higher they climbed. They neared the peak and were stopped behind several lorries parked on the steep incline, unable to continue because of ice on the road. Vlasta shared the rest of the story:

'I was in the front seat with a thermos in one hand, a cup in the other, enjoying some coffee, laughing and talking. Suddenly I realized the lorry about ten metres in front of us was starting to slide back. I didn't understand what was happening. Then I saw the driver and a passenger jump out and I realized the problem was serious. I didn't know what to do. I dropped the coffee and tried to open the door,' she told me, demonstrating with frantic hand gestures.

'It was my first time in the front and I couldn't get the door open. I realized it was too late. I closed my eyes and I said, "Jesus – help!" When I opened my eyes I saw the lorry stopped one metre away from us. The lorry driver was shaking when they brought him back a half-hour later. "I said goodbye to you and the lorry already,' he told us, "because a situation like this always ends up as a great catastrophe.'

'We knew that God was with us and we should continue.' They went on to help two Jewish families come out of that tense region. I have been amazed at the lengths to which the Holy Spirit would take our volunteers on behalf of the Jewish people – even at risk of their lives – and I am so thankful that all have returned well from their journeys.

The pioneering work in Armenia proved that there

were indeed Jews there who wanted to come to Israel. The Jewish Agency agreed to finance a second flight of 98 *olim* organized by Esther and friend, and Ebenezer then sponsored a third with 115 *olim* in December 1994.

I was there to meet this flight in Tel Aviv. Passengers straggled in, the men unshaven, tired but exhilarated. Elsa and I had visited Armenia the month before and I recognized many of the *olim*. There was such joy. It was a very emotional coming together. Many had tears in their eyes.

A highway had been blazed for the ancient Jewish community of this isolated country! We turned the work in Armenia over to members of the local church. They sent a steady stream of *olim* out to Odessa by air, where they joined sailings of the *Dmitry Shostakovich* which we renewed in 1995. By this point over 500 Jews had come out of Armenia – after we'd first been told there were none there! And when Bagrat uncovered an old Armenian telephone directory – which are few and far between in the former Soviet Union – he found over 1,500 families with Jewish names to contact. I have no doubt there are far more Jews hidden away in the former Soviet Union than the official statistics tell us. God knows His people. He will find them.

✣   ✣   ✣

Elsa and I planned to return to Armenia. We were in Moscow and the Israeli consul there was taken aback when I said, 'Tomorrow we fly to Armenia.'

'Are you sure?' he asked me. 'There is unrest there! I advise you not to go.'

Elections had just been held which many Armenians believed were fraudulent. Riot police used tear gas, water cannons, and shots in the air to drive back a crowd threatening to storm the parliament. But we made contact with the church in Armenia and learned they had obtained permission to hold a conference about Israel, and I was to speak. Elsa and I prayed and felt to go.

Everywhere were military and tanks, and we had no visas, but even the immigration officers made us feel welcome. We had a most marvelous time. The 320 seats were packed for the day-long conference, with a few standing in the rear. I asked how long I could speak. The pastor looked surprised and said, 'As long as you like.'

It was a dynamic meeting. They wanted to know more about Israel. When I shared about our work, they spontaneously took up a collection. Then at night, to close the conference, the senior pastor took the microphone. 'Now we will bless Gustav and Elsa.' They took up a love offering for us. I had tears in my eyes when I saw those who had nothing coming forward to give us money, pencils, rings, chocolates, whatever they had. Truly the Lord richly rewarded our obedience to go there.

In almost every church we have been privileged to visit in the former Soviet Union the pastor has readily given over the pulpit for me to give a teaching on Israel and to share the vision of Operation Exodus. They understand the Jews – like them they have suffered much, and so are willing to help. We even have some of these churches giving us a tithe of their meagre income.

It has been a double blessing for Elsa and me when we also find churches in the West whose pastor has taught his congregation God's end-time purposes for the people and land of Israel. But more often when I share silence falls over a congregation. They are not quite sure how to respond. Some say, 'We have never heard anything like that.' So I always endeavour to work with much Scripture, as in this way our own eyes were first opened to the place of Israel.

I was invited to speak at a mid-week meeting in a Lutheran church in Germany. After I shared the vision of Operation Exodus the pastor, in casual dress, came forward. I thought he would pray and dismiss the congregation. I was not a little surprised when he said with conviction, 'I have listened carefully, and feel I should say that what Mr Scheller shared was fulfilled when the Jews returned from Babylon. It is no longer a subject for our times.' It was quite an occasion for me, standing there in front of the congregation. I listened and said nothing. Years ago I would have argued. Unlike the limited return of the Jews from Babylon, this return is to be global and permanent, as portrayed, for example, in Ezekiel 37:21–28. But I have learned to let God be the one who justifies.

During a time of prayer and fasting the Lord showed me that *aliyah* can be compared with the parable of the prodigal son in Luke 15. The Jews in the land of the north are coming under increasing pressure: economic pressure, political pressure, anti-Semitism. They suffer! Like the prodigal son they realize it is better for them to go home.

And then God showed me His Father's heart. I want to tell you, it is a broken heart. I saw it so clearly; He is longing for His people to come home. He is on the lookout and says, 'Come My children, come now.'

And then He showed me the elder brother. We are the elder brother! The body of Christ. Because the overwhelming majority who live in the body of Christ do not care about God's chosen people, do not care what is happening with Israel. The Father is grieving over the attitude of the elder brother.

Many in the Church know that the Great Commission must be completed before the return of the Lord (Matthew 24:14). But if we do not also recognize the role of Israel as we enter the end times, we are only standing on one leg. We see from Acts 1:6 and 3:21 that Jesus will come when the kingdom is restored to Israel, to reign *upon the throne of David and over His kingdom* (Isaiah 9:7).

As I've been praying I feel the Lord is saying to me, 'Gustav, I have waited almost two thousand years for this time.' Now is the time. God in His infinite mercy has given us this glorious opportunity to help His chosen people return to the Promised Land. I believe with all my heart that our actions are recorded in heaven and will bring joy and happiness to the Father.

Chapter 8

'Proclaim, give praise, and say,
"O Lord, save your people,
The remnant of Israel!"
Behold, I will bring them from
the north country,
and gather them from the
ends of the earth.'

(Jeremiah 31:7–8)

Maria, one of our team members, had been speaking to me for some time about the Jews in yet another former Soviet republic, Kazakhstan. 'I don't want to know about Kazakhstan,' I told her. 'First we have to consolidate our existing work.' It is a huge country, bigger than all of western Europe, and predominantly Muslim. But Maria continued to nudge me about Ebenezer's involvement. Reluctantly I decided one day to add it to my prayer diary. As I was making the entry, I was not a little surprised to see it was on the day we were called to pray for this very nation.

Early in 1995 Elsa and I flew into the city of Karaganda, in the centre of Kazakhstan, on a propeller-driven Aeroflot aircraft. The hostess brought around drinks. It was only water, and in a not-very-appetizing plastic mug, which was then rinsed and reused for the other passengers. Strangely, food and drink do not seem to have the same importance to us as in the west. When we are on the Lord's assignments, we are consumed with our task. We joyfully accept food and living conditions that we would never put up with back home.

I must confess we sometimes call this company not Aeroflot, but 'Aeroflop'. As a frequent traveller on this airline, I could add many pages to this book sharing some of our eventful flight experiences. Let me just sum up ... flight delays, cancellation of actual flights and even closure of whole airports due to lack of fuel or weather conditions. None of these is unusual. Often there are extra passengers standing for the entire flight as paying guests of the captain! I jokingly enquire of my wife whether she has packed our screwdriver. We cover each flight in prayer, knowing that when we are in the perfect will of the Father there is no safer place for us on all the earth, even on an 'Aeroflop' plane.

As we stepped out of the aircraft in Karaganda, waiting for us on the tarmac was the leader of the Jewish community, Leonid, who later became a dear and trusted friend and a loyal representative of Ebenezer. At the end of our visit Leonid embraced me warmly, and said, 'One day my grandchildren will know that Gustav has come to Karaganda to call the Jews home to Israel.'

In our repeated visits, we have seen firsthand the survival battle of the people living in this harsh land.

Doctors, teachers and pensioners had not been paid for six to eight months. The infrastructure was collapsing – the electricity and water supplies were cut; there had been no cooking gas in the homes for a year and in severe weather conditions many homes and offices had no heating. By now many of the Jews realized it was time to leave. The Lord used this strong bond of friendship in the following year to bring out 1,000 *olim* from that mountainous land.

I can still see the face of a Jewish lady in her early 50s who had adopted three street children. She looked hopefully to me and said, 'I want to go home – but only if I can take these children with me.' For a fleeting moment I thought such a desire to be impossible. She had no documents. She had picked up these little children off the street and did not even know their full names. How would it be possible to secure Israeli visas in such circumstances?

It was many months later when our representative telephoned me and told me that this lady and her children would be on our next flight. Tears welled up in my eyes. God had again made the impossible possible.

During these months the shipping line continued to flourish, and when I was due to fly out to Odessa for the last sailing of 1995 I knew that I'd be put under extreme pressure. Our volunteers, our Israeli shipping partners, the owners of the *Dmitry Shostakovich*, and the owners of the transit camp in Odessa were all asking me, 'When will we sail again?'

But every time I inquired of the Lord I just couldn't

get an answer. The night before I cried out to the Lord, 'Give me a clear sign what to do!'

Elsa and I had to leave the next morning at 4:00 a.m. for Heathrow airport. When I awoke, to my amazement my otherwise reliable Swiss watch had come to a standstill – and my morning reading in *Daily Watchwords* was, *'Stand still and see the salvation of the Lord.'* I knew God had spoken, and it was no longer a problem for me. Some were disappointed, but I just knew we had to wait. I do not dare make a move until the time the Lord gives the revelation. If I go against what He has shown me, my life is not worth living.

At the same time we found that we did not have sufficient funds to pay the final sailing bill. God had always provided through the years chiefly by the small gifts of faithful believers, but now we came under increasing pressure. Elsa and I were considering selling our Swiss apartment, which we had bought some years earlier for our retirement and had paid for over a period of 20 years. Elsa, being a wise woman, said, 'Let's fast and pray for a week.'

I will never forget that after five days of fasting an excited Beverley telephoned me to say that Ebenezer had received a substantial legacy which would completely clear all our debts. We were overjoyed. It was as if the Lord gave us back our lovely apartment. Somehow I was reminded of Abraham, who put Isaac on the altar and God abundantly blessed him for it.

Then in early January I had the release that we would sail again and I could start my negotiations. 'Lord,' I prayed one morning at home, 'should we use the same vessel?' I jumped in my car to drive to the office and switched on the radio. Usually I listen to worship tapes, but I enjoyed the particular piece of classical music that was playing. The announcer came on and said, 'That was by Dmitry Shostakovich,' the Russian composer for whom the ship was named! I knew the Lord was saying to move ahead.

He knows the end from the beginning. On our return to Odessa we found that mighty BLASCO was now in such financial difficulty it had started to dispose of some of its passenger fleet. This created competition, as the new owners of these vessels were eager to do business with us. We were able to charter the *Dmitri Shostakovich* in 1996 on terms which saved money and made our lives easier than if we'd accepted the contract offered in December.

✤ ✤ ✤

Even though we were now established in three republics, I found my heart was still stirring with an impression: 'Go where no one else is going.' I knew that operations in difficult areas wouldn't bring back the majority of *olim* to Israel. But I began to see that Operation Exodus, as Johannes once put it, is more than anything else a prophetic sign. Our calling is to open the way like a plough, and bring back the most impossible cases.

I thought I'd test the waters when I saw the senior official for immigration at the Israeli embassy in Moscow. 'In which part of the former Soviet Union do Jews most need help to make *aliyah*?' I asked him.

'Siberia,' he answered without any hesitation. It struck a chord in my heart. A few weeks later I was at the Israeli embassy in Kiev, asked the same question and instantly received the same reply.

I remembered well the first time Elsa and I visited Siberia. Following the *Mediterranean Sky* sailings, the Lord had shown us to explore many parts of the former Soviet Union, and we travelled right through to the end of Siberia on board the trans-Siberia train.

On the first leg of our journey we sat on the hard wooden benches of an old second-class carriage from Riga to Minsk. It was approaching midnight and, forgive the expression, my bottom hurt a bit by that time. I was tired, and I looked at Elsa. And as I looked at my wife I started laughing. I couldn't stop it. I looked at her and she giggled as well. After a while I said, 'Either we are utterly mad or this is the Lord.'

After midnight we got to our hotel in Minsk. I had already gone to bed when the Lord reminded me that I hadn't done my evening reading. So I sat up, turned on the light and read that day's selection from 1 Corinthians 1:27:

> 'But God has chosen the foolish things of the world to put to shame the wise.'

It made me feel good!

> 'And God has chosen the weak things of this world to put to shame the things which are mighty.'

We spent eight days and nights on trains. It was bumpy. We couldn't read because the book would be shaking too much. It was best just to look out of the window. There was nothing to eat; we'd buy food when we stopped at a station for 15 minutes. When I stepped off the train I was never sure whether the platform was going up and down or if it was me! Poorly-dressed women would stand there with whatever they had to sell. I remember one woman selling mashed potatoes from a pot in her baby's pushchair. I caught her eye and saw desperation.

During this journey Elsa and I made a side trip to see the Jewish autonomous region created by Stalin back in 1928. He moved Jews to the far end of Siberia, on the border with China – the middle of nowhere. We felt to go there and visit the capital, Birobidzhan. It was quite an experience to pull into the train station and see the name of the city written in both Russian and Hebrew!

When we got there we had three addresses, possible contacts. At the first two places we couldn't find anybody. We went to the third one and it happened to be the leader of the entire Jewish community of the area. I shared my heart with him. He asked us to stay for a beautiful meal, and then he said, 'Tonight we are celebrating *Shavuot* at the synagogue. It will be packed. Will you come with us?' I had no idea. It was God's timing. The Lord had sent us all the way to the far end of Siberia exactly on that night when they would celebrate, when their little wooden synagogue would be full. And I had liberty that night to tell them, 'Now is the time to go home.'

We drew near the conclusion of our journey and were looking forward to flying to Japan the next day. Elsa and I must have spent about 200 hours on the train. Very often they played hard rock music in the coaches. It is good for headaches – it sounds as if it comes from the pits of hell. Suddenly the rock music went quiet. Then, in the last few minutes, they started to play Handel's beautiful 'Hallelujah Chorus'. We'd never heard anything like that. In the middle of Siberia, at the far end of the earth! It was as if the Lord was saying, 'Well done, my good and faithful servants.' We were in tears. It was such a beautiful experience.

✛ ✛ ✛

Three years later Elsa and I flew into Magadan, the city to the farthest east in Siberia, to begin our work in earnest. The territory is so vast – three times the size of the US continent – that our flight from Moscow lasted eight hours. Stalin sent millions to prison camps at Magadan precisely for its isolation. It is accessible only by air, boat, or, in season, a four-wheel-drive vehicle carrying its own fuel supply across dirt roads and ferries. No walls or guards were needed here – there was nowhere to flee.

Countless millions perished in the Siberian gulag. Many of these were Jews and Christians sent away for practising their faith. For me this is the place nearest to hell on earth. And as Elsa and I looked at the run-down shacks and rubbish lying about, we could sense a depression, like a spirit of death which still hovered over the area.

We felt prompted in our spirits to go on a prayer walk through parts of the city. We set out on a cold summer day. Patches of snow were still on the nearby mountain tops. We came to a high point directly overlooking the harbour, where ships had brought in the prisoners destined to die. It just gripped me, such a sense that the Lord was saying, 'Prophesy over this city.'

It was something I had never done. As we stood there Ezekiel's vision of dry bones came to me. I opened my Bible to Ezekiel 37:12 and spoke out the words:

> *'Thus says the Lord GOD: "Behold, O My people, I will open your graves and cause you to come up from your graves, and bring you into the land of Israel."'*

I was deeply stirred. Tears came to my eyes. I just knew at that moment that the Lord was calling us to call forth his sons and daughters from the ends of the earth.

Elsa and I were invited to dinner in Magadan with a Jewish woman, her son and his young wife. This family had so little. But the mother worked for two days to prepare a beautiful meal. She put mountains of food on the table. We felt embarrassed. It was much more than we could eat.

After the meal, as our hostess poured us steaming sweet tea, I pulled out my weapon, the Bible. 'Look what Moses said 3,000 years ago,' I told them, turning to Deuteronomy 30:4:

> *'If any of you are driven out to the farthest parts under heaven, from there the LORD your God will gather you.'*

I paused and looked them in the eyes. 'You live in the farthest part of the earth and it is time to go home.'

I'll never forget I was in Odessa for our first sailing of 1996 and the son and his wife turned up! 'You know,' he told me, 'when you spoke about going home to Israel I knew it was time.' They sold everything and flew to Moscow to have their papers approved by the Israeli embassy. But their plane broke down; they were left to walk long hours through the snow; they were attacked and robbed of all their money; even some of their belongings were stolen on the train to Odessa. By the time we met them they were devastated. But our people just loved them. When I said goodbye to them as they left to board the ship, there was new hope.

We put together a team to fish for more families like this one, and help them with a safe, reliable route to Israel. We met in early 1996 in Khabarovsk, the capital of eastern Siberia, for a week of prayer and discussion, a time of mapping out our strategic plans. Our volunteers were to fan out from there in twos to spy out the land, pray, and prophetically call forth the Jews.

The day before they were to leave I was privileged to speak at the local Bible school, and I shared that we were sending out fishing teams. There were students attending who had come from the various regions. A young man came forward. 'I can help your people to find the Jews in my city.' Others followed his lead. I could see the relief on the faces of our volunteers, who otherwise would have journeyed to these distant places knowing not a soul. This is not Europe or the

United States. This is the end of the earth where communication is often complicated or even non-existent, and foreigners are watched with suspicion.

The students immediately made contact with their home churches, and all our volunteers were met on their arrival with a bed and food provided. Truly the Lord is the best administrator! Rarely have I felt His presence and love so much as out in that forsaken land.

Our volunteers returned with glorious stories of how God cares and makes a way to reach these isolated Jews. Yveta, a Czech girl who with her friend Martina was a pioneer of our work in Siberia, told of her visit to a remote settlement:

'I had a prompting. The Lord told me to leave Magadan and go into the interior. I wanted to visit a settlement 600 kilometres north. There is a minibus service, a weekly one which goes high into the interior only on dirt roads. When you drive there it is so unreal, you just glide. You hold on because everything shakes all the time. The roads are full of holes.

We were about 300 kilometres inland when the minibus broke down. When we opened the door hundreds of big mosquitoes came in and they were really hungry. I had never seen so many and such big mosquitoes in my life. The driver shook his head and said that he couldn't repair the vehicle, and I knew we would be stranded for days before anyone found us. I prayed to the Lord, "Will You make a way?"

Suddenly the driver looked up and said, "I have an idea." Within half an hour we drove on. When we got to the settlement it was like a miracle, an oasis in the middle of nowhere. There was a church and through them I found more than 30 Jewish families. Some of them had never heard anything like it when I came and said, "It's time to go home. The God of Israel, His plans for you are good. You have a future." They knew about Israel, but didn't see how they could ever make it there. We told them we would help them.

Some were so surprised that we could find them, because they never told anybody they were Jewish and thought nobody in the settlement knew – but people knew very well who was who. One Jewish lady was in shock when I found her and did not want to speak with me. She was closing the door and saying, "No, no, no."

Then I prayed, "Lord, would you see that we have a good journey back?" Many gold mines are in this area which were once worked by prisoners. We came to a working gold mine and the manager said, "I need to go back to Magadan with my helicopter. I will give you a ride." And in two hours I was back in Magadan.'

It's not an easy thing to help Jews in these remote areas. Just to get a photograph of them, to get their documents checked, or to get a passport can be an overwhelming task. It is a long-term process. In some cases we must send them to other republics to research their family history and obtain proof of their Jewishness.

In our first two years of fishing in eastern Siberia we saw over two thousand *olim* leave for Israel. We brought them by air, bus or train – often hazardous and difficult journeys – to a small hotel in Khabarovsk where they were secure while waiting for a Jewish Agency flight. I'll always remember one little lady on crutches I met there. She was about 4ft 6ins. The team said to me, 'Gustav, you must meet her, she is a special lady.' And then they whispered to me, 'She knows the Lord.'

They wanted to take a photo of us. She said, 'I am too small. Let's stand next to the staircase.' So she climbed up on the first step and said, 'I'm still too small.' She climbed up to the second step so she was on the same level with me. We photographed and had a glorious time. She was 81 years old and had practically no teeth, but her eyes were shining. She wanted to go home.

Our research has shown that there are thousands more Jews in the Far East, from Magadan right up to the Bering Straits. A vast territory! Many Jews came as prisoners, and the survivors and their families continue to live there in exile. They often hide their Jewishness, making it impossible to know how many remain. Only now are they coming out and confessing as a way of escape.

So often humanitarian aid is the key to get in these places and get a response. We've had 40–foot containers sent in from western Europe and the United States. When we visit synagogues and tell the rabbi we want to share the vision of Operation Exodus only a small number of Jews turn up. But if we say we are bringing aid to his people we know that they will all turn up and it gives us opportunity to speak about going home.

One volunteer asked me, 'Would you like to visit the poorest of the poor?' I said, 'Yes,' though I don't find it easy to go into these homes to see utter misery. We drove there with our minibus and what moved my heart is that the children and the old ones came running out and embraced our volunteer. They had become friends and she said, 'Gustav, I have gained their confidence, now I am going to talk to them and tell them that it is time to go home.'

It is not easy to earn the trust of the Russian Jews. It takes time. It takes real commitment. I always say to our volunteers, 'Love never fails.' And so we break first into fallow ground, we water it, and many times the Lord allows us to bring in the harvest.

✤ ✤ ✤

From Siberia Elsa and I continued eastward by air to Alaska. It was a glorious day and I took in the snow-peaked mountains, glaciers, and valleys during the six-hour flight. It reminded me of a vision numerous believers have shared that one day large numbers of Jews will travel over this forsaken land, across the Bering Straits into Alaska.

Elsa was sitting behind me, also in a window seat, spying out the terrain from the air. The longer she looked the more she doubted that such a land route could be possible. 'There would be elderly people, children, invalids,' she thought. 'Wild animals inhabit the region such as Siberian tigers, bears, and wolves.' 'Lord,' she said in her spirit, 'if this is of you please give me a sign.'

As she continued to look out she saw a picture formed by the mountains, valleys, and crevices below. It was a large eagle with outstretched wings. Suddenly she remembered God's word to Moses in Exodus 19:4:

> *'You have seen what I did to the Egyptians, and how I bore you on eagles' wings and brought you to Myself.'*

As I write we are investigating the possibility of bringing the first *olim* out through Alaska by air. I had the joy of speaking in a church in Alaska and sharing the possibility of an exodus across the Bering Straits. It was another of those electric meetings. The pastor came forward and said, 'We as a church have already made preparations to welcome the Jews when they come.'

Could circumstances really require such an escape route? I learned one lesson on our first trans-Siberian train journey that I've never forgotten. It happened on the border of Mongolia. The train came to a stop in a town called Chita. I asked Elsa to buy some bread while I wanted to take a few camera shots. I had two small cameras, one for prints and one for slides. As I was taking these pictures I saw that my wife couldn't get anywhere near this wooden stall. Everybody was pushing. We were not in Britain there! And so I came and used my elbows, I admit, more effectively. I got to the front and put my cameras down to pay for the bread when I realized our train was slowly moving out of the station. In this part of the country a passenger train leaves only every three days. Elsa and I started running. We caught up to a rear compartment of the train, climbed on, and made our way forward to our own car. I settled down holding the two loaves of bread. 'Oh, **no**!' I cried. 'I've left the cameras behind.'

I was furious with myself. Both cameras gone! So I went to find an Intourist guide on the train and asked whether there was a lost and found office to report it. She laughed. 'Something like that doesn't exist in Russia.'

As I was still brooding over my loss the Lord spoke to me and said, 'So it will be with the Jews who are not going now. They will run for their lives and leave everything behind.' Even as we continue our fishing work I believe that the time of the hunters is near, as so clearly portrayed in Jeremiah 16:16.

Kjell told me he was praying aloud about our work as he walked in the Swedish forest. Suddenly a hunter turned up. 'Would you please be quiet!' he scolded. 'You're disturbing the animals.' Kjell saw it as a prophetic signal.

Anti-Semitism is not over. A young Jewish man we were helping to make *aliyah* in far-eastern Siberia was murdered six days before he was due to fly to Tel Aviv. A month previously the couple heading the Jewish Agency office in another Siberian city were badly beaten and robbed by men who told them, 'You have paid for your guilt to Russia – now you can go to Israel.' Our team helped them leave six days later.

Ultra-nationalist groups are openly inciting against the Jews in Siberia. I have seen signs on walls in cities, I have seen newspapers where they call for the extinction of the Jews. I have a strong sense we are in a countdown. This is born out by many of our intercessors, who have picked up in the Spirit that we are headed for turbulent times. The Lord has imprinted on us Zechariah 2:6:

'Up, up! Flee from the land of the north!'

One night in our Bournemouth office the clock fell from the wall, smashed to the floor, and stopped working, the hands pointing at less than two minutes before midnight. We keep it as a reminder.

Sometimes we have tried to convey this to the Jews. Many were not ready to accept it. It's a human trait to hope that things will get better. Many told us, 'I will be the last one to go.' When Elsa told our Jewish partners in Odessa that the empty cabins on the 1993 sailings could mean Jewish lives one day, they thought she was over the top. Zionist activist Vladimir Jabotinsky received the same response when he attempted to warn European Jews in the 1930s.

Not only in Alaska, but as I have travelled throughout North America and Europe, I have come across churches, fellowships, and individual believers who are making physical preparation to help the Jews on their way home. A friend shared a dream in which he saw how the Jews were persecuted, how they could not even escape from one country to the next. He saw bloodshed and terrible scenes. There was only one safe destination – Israel.

When he woke he wept before the Lord and asked why there was no one to help His people. The Lord showed him a big world map with many little flashing lights, and he realized these were the Bible-believing Christians who would help the Jewish people on their way home.

In our generation, as in the Holocaust, Christians may once again be challenged to lay down their lives for the kinsfolk of Messiah. *'Inasmuch as you did it to one of the least of these My brethren,'* the King will answer us one day, *'you did it to Me.'*

Not the Final Chapter!

Gustav Scheller lived to see Ebenezer complete a hundred Operation Exodus sailings. Sadly, he wasn't aboard the *Dmitry Shostakovich* when the Ukrainian ship docked at Haifa on 8th December 1999 at the end of that historic trip which brought 379 more Jewish immigrants back to the land of their fore-fathers, but he was full of joy when he spoke via a telephone link-up later that day from his hospital bed in England to a celebration in Jerusalem. 'I am so grateful to the Lord for the way He led us to expand the work of Ebenezer step by step,' he told leaders, volunteers, national co-ordinators and supporters. Reflecting on Ebenezer's phenomenal growth, Gustav declared: 'It is God's doing and I want to give Him all the honour and all the glory.' He rejoiced over the Lord's provision of the necessary resources at the right time, especially personnel and finances: 'He is truly the best administrator.'

Significantly, the gathering took place in the same basement room at the Holyland Hotel where Ebenezer and Operation Exodus had been born in January 1991.

As Gustav's voice rang out it was the last time many of the listeners heard him. Just a few weeks later he made his own *aliyah* – to Heaven.

The centenary voyage reflected the comparatively trouble-free operation the sailings had become since Gustav took the huge step of faith in hiring the *Mediterranean Sky* for three initial sailings so fraught with difficulties.

Over 21,000 Jews from many parts of the former Soviet Union made *aliyah* with Ebenezer's help during the centenary sailing year. Thousands more have done so since. Ebenezer has opened more offices across this vast territory and gained more help from fSU churches – backed by an increasing number of national co-ordinators around the world. Many Jews have gone to Israel literally from 'the ends of the earth' – Siberia and the Russian Far East. 'Please do not underestimate the value of your work. Virtually no one goes home from this region without having been helped by Ebenezer,' stated the Sochnut (Jewish Agency) director for the region.

In the months leading up to the centenary sailing teams started to help Jews go home to Israel from Turkmenistan and Tajikistan, which meant that Ebenezer was working in the whole of Muslim-dominated Central Asia. In Kazakhstan, the biggest country in an area covering 5.8 million square miles, teams range far and wide from the main base in Almaty, often travelling 20 hours and more by train to find Jews and urge them to go home. Increasingly the message is backed up by distribution of humanitarian aid – food, clothing, medicines and even special items such as hearing aids. This Christian love in action has made a deep impact among God's ancient people.

The centenary sailing year also saw Operation Exodus begin in Moldova and Belarus, the two countries in the western part of the former Soviet Union where Jews, along with those in Ukraine, suffered horrendously during the Holocaust. In Belarus, which has remained a staunch Communist country despite the collapse of the Soviet empire, Ebenezer helped nearly 1,300 Jews to reach the Promised Land within the first six months of setting up base in Minsk and the work has gone from strength to strength since then. Operation Exodus began in Moldova three months later and hundreds of Jews have since reached Israel by Jewish Agency flights or by being bussed by Ebenezer to join the ship in Odessa.

Jews in Armenia, a country especially dear to Gustav's heart, have continued to make *aliyah* with the help of Ebenezer's dedicated team there. Operation Exodus began in neighbouring Georgia in 1998. There are many more Jews in the land of Stalin's birth than there are in Armenia and the work has been making a deep impact among them. Training local Christians to 'fish' for Jews has been a priority and, with strong prayer backing in the churches, teams regularly collect Jews and transport them by minibus to Tbilisi for Jewish Agency flights to Tel Aviv. In Georgia, as in other parts of the former Soviet Union, the teams' love, expressed practically through aid distribution to the poor and needy, has brought the

traditional walls between Christians and Jews crash-
ing down.

One rabbi wasn't interested in meeting an Operation Exodus team. He wanted nothing to do with
Christians. But on the road from Tbilisi to Batumi,
capital of the autonomous republic of Atchara, along
Georgia's south-western border with Turkey, the team
phoned him again. This time the answer was different: Yes, they could come to his home for ten
minutes. He was waiting for them with his wife and
children. No sooner had they sat down than the
questions began: 'I have heard about your work.
Why are you Christians helping Jews?' Theo told
him that it is written in the *Tenakh* that a massive
exodus, far greater than the one from Egypt, would
take place – and non-Jews would help in this. Today
God, not Ebenezer, was gathering His people. The
questions continued to come thick and fast until
the rabbi, suddenly softening, said: 'You and your
workers are welcome in our home any time. You
really have a divine task.' The ten-minute meeting
had lasted an hour and a half. God had arranged it.

A significant advancement came with the establishment of Ebenezer in Moscow in 2000. Soon Jews
living in the capital were being helped to make *aliyah*
and Operation Exodus teams were breaking new
ground in the Russian Federation. Dagestan, the
mountainous Caucasian republic on the Caspian
Sea, is one of the most recent areas where Moscow
team members got work started.

During 2000 Ebenezer set up an intensive training
programme in eastern Ukraine for local Christians to

help spread the vision of making *aliyah* among the 40,000 Jews living in Donetsk Oblast, the country's mining heartland.

While seeking to bring as many Jews out of the former Soviet Union as possible (it was estimated that around 1.5 million still lived there in 2000), Ebenezer remains true to God's calling to find Jews in special need of help to go to the Promised Land – particularly the poor, the sick and those who live in remote areas. Jews like Viktor Osadchi. The widower in his fifties was scraping an existence for himself and his three children by looking after deer in the harsh Chukotskiy region in the far north of Siberia when Sergey and Zhenya, a young couple serving as Ebenezer volunteers, met him. As they told him of the opportunity to make a new start in the land of his ancestors hope dawned in Viktor's heart. His life had been one of dashed hopes and tragedy, culminating in his wife dying through vodka addiction. He and his children were existing on dry bread when the volunteers found him. Ebenezer took care of all their needs, including apartment rental and new clothes, while the process to gain the necessary documents to make *aliyah* moved to completion. Today they are in the Promised Land.

Jews like Spartyak Rabiev. He was desperate to leave Tajikistan. His sister had made *aliyah* in 1993 and the rest of the family was ready to follow. But business was good for the father and he kept saying, 'Wait a little. We will soon go.' One day they found him in the street – murdered. Seventeen-year-old Spartyak himself ended up in hospital after being beaten by men shouting at him to stop being a Jew and become a Muslim. Ebenezer's advancement into the country resulted in Spartyak, and other Tajik Jews, being helped to reach Israel.

God has been preparing Ebenezer to help greater numbers of Jews to make *aliyah*. A new, long-term shipping contract was recently signed and *The Iris*, sister ship of the *Russ*, which was used for most of 2000, is due to start bringing Jews from Odessa to Haifa in spring 2001. She will have double the capacity of her predecessor. Ebenezer is stepping up efforts to seek out Jews while the doors remain open to do so – continuing to do the work Gustav Scheller began in obedience to God's calling.

In the first seven years of Operation Exodus nearly 20,000 Jews were helped to reach Israel. Since then another 50,000 have been helped to do so. But Gustav pointed out that 'one day the Church shall see the much greater fruit of the final world-wide return' – a regathering that would be followed by the return of Jesus Christ, the Messiah. It was this greater return that Gustav had in mind when he spoke to the centenary celebration in Jerusalem: 'At present our work is, rightly, concentrated on the land of the north. With the economic breakdown and growing anti-Semitism it is likely that doors will close before very long. I hardly need to remind you that many more Jews are living in the West. I believe the work of Ebenezer has just begun!'

Appendix 1

Text of letter from Dr Kingsley Priddy of the Bible College of Wales:

At Eastbourne
22.ix.94

My dear Gustav and Elsa,

...God, the Holy Spirit, is in 'Operation Exodus' in an unique way. It is His own intercessory ministry for the return to Israel of the world's Jews. It is He who through this ministry is gaining a position of intercession which will prevail for the return of the ultimate remnant that is to be brought back from the four corners of the earth...

I remember your asking me some time ago to put something in writing with regard to the intercessory nature of 'Operation Exodus'. I did give some time to it then but somehow it never 'took off'; the Spirit did not give the liberty then, but I believe that now is His time.

You see, Intercession is not prayer, nor even very intense prayer. Anyone may pray, and pray earnestly, for something, and yet not be committed to be irrevocably responsible, at any cost, for its fulfilment. The intercessor is.

In Intercession there is Identification with the matter or persons interceded for. The intercessor is willing to take the place of the one prayed for; to let **their** need become **his** need; to let **their** need be met at **his** expense and to let **their** suffering become the travail of **his** own heart.

That is how the Lord Jesus *'made intercession for the transgressors'* (Isaiah 53:12). *'He was numbered with the transgressors,'* and *'He was wounded for* (their) *transgressions'* (v. 5). He had to be 'identified' with sinners; He secured their pardon by vicariously paying the debt that they owed.

He even went so far as to be *'made sin'* for us that we might be righteous in God's sight. He had to encounter everything that could ever come against us in the way of temptation, satanic opposition and such trials as abound in a fallen world. Whatever the devil was capable of he had to be free to bring it against the Lord Jesus. Jesus said to him, represented in his agents, *'This is your hour'* (Luke 22:53) when they came to arrest him.

'In all things He had to be made like His brethren ... to make propitiation for the sins of the people. For in that He himself has suffered being tempted, He is able to aid those who are tempted' (Hebrews 2:17–18).

And because *'the wages of sin is death,'* He had to partake of our flesh and blood *'that through death He might destroy him who had the power of death, that is, the devil, and release those who through fear of death were all their lifetime subject to bondage'* (Hebrews 2:14–15).

Only by such identification with sinners, even to suffering the very ultimate consequences of sin, in faultless victory, did our Lord gain that place of intercession for sinners which enabled Paul to throw out the challenge: *'Who is he who condemns? It is Christ who died, and is risen, who is even at the right hand of God, who also makes intercession for us'* (Romans 8:34).

And we are assured in Hebrews 7:25 that *'He is able to save to the uttermost those who come to God through Him, since He ever lives to make intercession for them.'*

The nearest anyone came to such a position under the Old Covenant was Moses, when he offered, if Israel's sin could be forgiven in no other way, to take their place and let God's judgment fall upon him. *'If you will forgive their sin – but if not, I pray, blot me out of your book which you have written'* (Exodus 32:32).

Others of the prophets became so identified with the nation that they could truly intercede for it. Even when Jeremiah felt the burden of the nation to be so heavy that he could never prophesy to it again, he found himself so in the grip of it, as fire shut up in his bones, that he could not hold it back (Jeremiah 20:8–9). Jeremiah was so identified with the nation that when, after the destruction of Jerusalem, the king of Babylon offered Jeremiah his liberty and protection, he chose to stay to minister to the remnant that were left, even when they disregarded the Lord's instructions and went off to Egypt (Jeremiah 43:4–7).

Esther was an intercessor when she laid her own life on the line, if by so doing her people might be saved (Esther 4:16).

Daniel's identification with the nation is clearly seen in Daniel 9 when everything else was put aside that he might cry to God for their return to their own land, in accordance with Jeremiah's prophecy. Not only did he prevail in this so that God was able to move Cyrus to fulfil it, but he had entered a spiritual realm in which God was able to reveal to him mysteries concerning the coming of Messiah and His atoning sacrifice (vv. 20–27).

But mostly God looked in vain for such people. *'He saw that there was no man, and wondered that there was no intercessor'* (Isaiah 59:16). At a later time He said, *'I sought for a man among them who would make a wall, and stand in the gap before me on behalf of the land ... but I found no one'* (Ezekiel 22:30).

In this dispensation it is the Holy Spirit Himself who is the true intercessor on earth. *'The Spirit himself makes intercession for us with groanings which cannot be uttered ... He makes intercession for the saints according to the will of God'* (Romans 8:26–27).

But He has limited Himself to exercising this ministry through redeemed men (or women) who have allowed Him to indwell their bodies as His temples (1 Corinthians 6:19). He would be quenched if there were any tension or conflict between His will and theirs, which necessitates such a surrender of the believer's will that his body can be presented to God as *'a living sacrifice'* (Romans 12:1).

Then there is a daily dying to self-will that the Holy Spirit may be free to live **His** life within that body. As Paul said, *'We who live are always delivered to death for Jesus' sake, that the life of Jesus may be manifested in our mortal flesh. So then* *death is working in us, but life in you'* (2 Corinthians 4:11–12). It is a costly, but glorious, ministry.

So the human channel becomes increasingly identified with the indwelling Spirit, as they both jointly become identified with the one for whom intercession is being made.

The pain and trials that are experienced are partly because thereby the natural life still remaining in the human instrument – elements of pride, selfishness, stubbornness, jealousy etc. – may be put to death, *'crucified with Christ'* (Galatians 2:20), and be replaced by *'the new man, created according to God in righteousness and true holiness'* (Ephesians 4:24).

God's way is always the way of the cross for it is only through death that resurrection life can be realised. *'Unless an ear of wheat falls into the ground and dies, it remains alone; but if it dies, it produces much fruit'* (John 12:24).

Even in a matter which has been given by God and is in accordance with the will of God, if great success and prosperity follow it is impossible for the human instrument not to take some pride or credit, even if only in thought, unless that element in him has truly died. That is why it seems to be inevitable that at some stages the work of God will seem to go to death, that the one to be used will know truly what an inadequate failure he is and then, when God ultimately brings resurrection and gives the victory, His channel will never touch the glory even in thought.

But pain and trials are also experienced because the accomplishing of God's will is always opposed by the devil. His agents will certainly contest the work of God and use every means available to do so.

The Spirit through His instruments must repel and defeat every such attack by laying hold of Calvary's once-and-for-all victory and applying it through faith and obedience, using *'the sword of the Spirit, which is the word of God.'* As the enemy is overcome at every point a victory is established which can subsequently be applied again in similar circumstances. This is gaining a position of intercession from which intercession may be made in future.

Thus it is that, from His once-and-for-all victory gained at Calvary, the Lord Jesus *'ever lives to make intercession for'* every sinner who will come to God through Him.

It is in such a manner that the Holy Spirit is using 'Operation Exodus' to gain a position of intercession for the subsequent return of the Jews from every part of the world. Although that is clearly foretold in Scripture and is certain of fulfilment, it will not happen automatically.

God foretold through Jeremiah that the Jews would return from Babylon after seventy years, but it necessitated the intercession of Daniel when that time came to bring its fulfilment.

Although our Lord said that *'this gospel of the kingdom will be preached in all the world as a witness to all the people groups'* before the end will come, the Holy Spirit will not be able to do that without the lives of multitudes of the saints being sacrificially placed at His disposal.

In the course of 'Operation Exodus' the devil must be allowed to bring every kind of opposition against it that he can devise. But as, through faith and costly obedience by His channels, the Holy Spirit overcomes every one of these, every weapon that the enemy could use to prevent the full second exodus from taking place will already have been blunted or broken. So he will be powerless to prevent that mighty surge of the Spirit when His time comes to complete His final *aliyah* from the four quarters of the globe ...

It is a great privilege, but a very costly one, for Gustav and Elsa, and all who will be 100% involved with them, to be the Holy Spirit's prepared instruments for this end-time intercessory ministry. They will need and deserve all the support that the rest of us can give in prayer and other ways. *Shalom!*

Yours in His love and triumph,

Kingsley

Appendix 2

Bible References

Prophecies of God's Word:

Genesis 12:1–3
Genesis 35:11–12
Jeremiah 23:3–7
Jeremiah 30:10

Ezekiel 20:33–35
Ezekiel 36:17–28
Zephaniah 2:1–2

Performance of God's Word:

Isaiah 49:22
Isaiah 59:21
Jeremiah 31:37
Ezekiel 36

Romans 11:11–12, 17–18,
25–31
Romans 15:27
Ephesians 3:6

General References for further study:

Deuteronomy 4:27
Deuteronomy 28:64a
Deuteronomy 30:1–4
Deuteronomy 32:26
Psalm 105:37, 42–43
Psalm 106:44–47
Psalm 122:6
Psalm 137:4–6
Psalm 147:1–2
Isaiah 11:10–12
Isaiah 14:1–2
Isaiah 27:12–13
Isaiah 36:8–10
Isaiah 40:1–5
Isaiah 41:8–11
Isaiah 42:22
Isaiah 43:1, 2, 6, 8, 13
Isaiah 44:3–6
Isaiah 45:2–6
Isaiah 46:3–4

Isaiah 49:8–10
Isaiah 51:14
Isaiah 57:14, 18
Isaiah 60:4, 8–9
Isaiah 62:4–7, 10–12
Jeremiah 13:16–18
Jeremiah 16:14–16
Jeremiah 23:3, 7–8
Jeremiah 30:16–17
Jeremiah 31:7–11, 31–34
Ezekiel 34:11–13, 16
Ezekiel 36:8, 24–28
Ezekiel 37:12–14
Ezekiel 39:27–28
Hosea, chapters 3, 4, 11, 14
Amos 9:11–14
Micah 4:6–7
Zephaniah 2:6–7
Romans 15:27

Appendix 3

Letters from the Knesset and Jewish Agency

IMMIGRATION & ABSORPTION
COMMITTEE

הכנסת
KNESSET

Jerusalem, 20 January 1992
15 Shevat 5752

Ebenezer Emergency Fund
EXODUS II
Ebenezer House
5a Poole Road
Bournemouth
ENGLAND

Dear Friends,

I have followed with great interest the establishment of the
EXODUS SHIPPING LINE. On behalf of the Immigration and Absorption
Committee of the Knesset, I am extending to you our sincere
congratulations on the successful completion of the first three
sailings from Odessa to Haifa.

I am well aware of all your efforts which have made these
historic sailings possible and I have been deeply touched by the
generous donations from Christians around the world. It is good to
see Israel has so many friends who care about the return of our people
from the land of the North.

My good wishes accompany EEF/EXODUS II, and may, through your
efforts, many thousands of Soviet Jews find their way home.

Yours sincerely,

Michael Kleiner, M.K.
Chairman

הסוכנות היהודית לארץ־ישראל
The Jewish Agency for Israel

המחלקה לעליה וקליטה

Department of Immigration

and Absorption

August 19, 1993

2 7 AUG 1993

Mr. Gustav Scheller
International Coordinator
Ebenezer Emergency Fund
Ebenezer House
5a Poole Road
Bournemouth BH2 5QJ
ENGLAND

Dear Mr. Scheller,

I was very impressed with your personality and your words at
the Knesset in Jerusalem. We very much appreciate what you
are doing for the Jewish people and the State of Israel.

I would also like to extend our appreciation to your sponsors.
You are part of a great historic event, the ingathering of the
Jewish people to their land. Thank you for what you are
doing.

Very truly yours,

Uri Gordon

Uri Gordon
Head, Department of
Immigration and Absorption

JERUSALEM, P.O.B. 92 ת"ד ירושלים
Tel: 02-202537-8 טל׳   Fax: 02-202251 פקס.
TEL-AVIV, 17 Kaplan Street – Tel. 03-5423450-690 טל׳ – 17 קפלן רח׳ תל־אביב,

Appendix 4

Getting involved

Is God calling you to be involved in Operation Exodus? One of the ways is to become a volunteer.

Barry Stronge is one of many who have done so. His testimony shows how the Lord can use us to help the Jews return to the Promised Land and, through this, prepare the way for Messiah's return:

'The young man on the quayside stopped waving because the ship had almost left harbour. He had said goodbye to his parents, perhaps forever, and was having difficulty in holding back his tears.

"You should be getting ready to go as well," I said.

"I can't go," he responded. "My wife is not Jewish and her parents are elderly. Why should we leave them?"

"Because the God of Israel is calling you," I answered.

"It doesn't apply to me," he said. "I've never been to a synagogue and I know nothing of religion."

I opened my Bible at Ezekiel 34 and read aloud:

> *"For thus says the Lord God: 'Indeed I myself will search for My sheep and seek them out. As a shepherd seeks out his flock on the day he is among his scattered sheep, so will I seek out My sheep and deliver them from all the places where they were scattered on a cloudy and dark day. And I will bring them out from the peoples and gather them from the countries, and will bring them to their own land . . . '"*

"It doesn't depend on what you may or may not have had the opportunity to learn. It depends only on the Word of God, who promises to take you home," I explained.

"But I don't know God," the young man protested.

"God knows you and is speaking to you," I declared.

The miracle loses nothing of its wonder in the repetition. It is the most awesome thing I have known: to look into the eyes of a son of Jacob and catch the moment when for the first time he **knows** he is hearing the God of Israel. He had been brought up in a society that had tried its utmost to abolish all concept of God. He may never have been in a synagogue or have little idea of who Abraham and Moses were. He believes he cannot know God because he has not been taught religion. But the God of Israel speaks directly to his heart and when he hears it he does not question its source. From that moment the issue of his repatriation is no longer a question of living space, economics or employment opportunities. His life, like the ship he had been watching depart, is on a new and irrevocable compass bearing.'

Ebenezer needs volunteers to serve for a minimum of three months in the former Soviet Union. Those fluent in Russian are especially needed. For further information about becoming a volunteer, and how to support the ongoing work of Operation Exodus through prayer and financial giving, please contact the nearest office – details can be found on the next page.

UK (Head Office)
Ebenezer Emergency Fund
Ebenezer House
5a Poole Road
Bournemouth BH2 5QJ

Tel: 01202 294455
Fax: 01202 295550
Email: enquiries@ebenezer-ef.org
Website: www.ebenezer-ef.org

USA
Ebenezer Emergency Fund
'Operation Exodus'
PO Box 26
162 Griggs Acres Road
Point Harbor
NC 27964-0026

Tel: 252 491 9201
Fax: 252 491 9202
Email: eefusa@juno.com

Canada
Ebenezer Emergency Fund
Ste. 414
151 10090 152 Street
Surrey
BC V3R 8X8

Tel: 604 572 2816
Fax: 604 583 6746
Email: wgamble@intergate.ca

Australia
EEF Australia
GPO Box 1950
Canberra
ACT 2601

Tel: 2 6257 8733
Fax: 2 6257 8735
Email: eefa@dingoblue.net.au

New Zealand
Ebenezer Emergency Fund
PO Box 5319
Terrace End
Palmerston North

Tel: 6 357 4883
Fax: 6 355 0037
Email: ebenezernz@xtra.co.nz

If you have enjoyed this book and would like to help us to
send a copy of it and many other titles to needy pastors in the
Third World, please write for further information
or send your gift to:

Sovereign World Trust
PO Box 777, Tonbridge, Kent TN11 0ZS
United Kingdom

or to the **'Sovereign World'** distributor
in your country.

Visit our website at www.sovereign-world.org
for a full range of Sovereign World books.